# TABLE OF CONTENTS

# ACRONYMS

AMISOM      African Union Mission for Somalia.

ARPCT       Alliance for Restoration of Peace and Counterterrorism.

ARS         Alliance for the Reliberation of Somalia.

ASWJ        Ahlu Suna Wal Jama'a.

AU          African Union.

CNRS        Centre Nationale de la Recherche Scientifique.

GWOT        Global War On Terror.

SICC        Supreme Islamic Courts Council.

SNIF        Somali National Islamic Front.

SOMA        Status Mission Agreement.

SPM         Somali Patriotic Movement.

SSDF        Somali Salvation Democratic Front.

TFG         Transitional Federal Government.

TNG         Transitional National Government.

UIC         Union of Islamic Court.

UN          United Nations.

USC         Union of Somali Congress.

# CHAPTER 1

## INTRODUCTION

### Background

Somalia became independent on July 1960 after the merger of the former British colony of Somaliland in the North and the Italian administered territory under UN mandate in the south. The country had experienced a democratic regime until 1969, when a military coup brought an army senior officer, Mohamed Siad Barre to power. As mentioned by Terrence Lyons and Ahmed I. Samatar, Barre introduced a vigorous program based on "scientific socialism" with a strong nationalistic flavor which ensured him the support of an enthusiastic population.[1] In the early years of the "kacaan" (revolution) the Somali population was supportive because they were tired of the unfruitful and corrupt politicians of the previous parliamentary regime.

As criticism started to rise, in particularly after the military defeat in the Ogaden War against Ethiopia in 1977, Barre tightened his grip and while brutally repressing any opposition he voluntarily used a clan based policy in order to divide people and preempt any serious opposition. This deliberate use by Barre of a clan based policy and the abuses of his regime are well reported in an Africa Watch Report published in January 1990.[2] In this document Barre's policy is thoroughly analyzed and a number of abuses and crimes committed by his regime are documented. It is noticeable that most of the atrocities took place in the North. Barre was from the south as were the majority of the members of his security apparatus. These divisive and unfortunate policies resulted in the decision of Somaliland to seek recognition as an independent state and refusal of any prospect of reunification with the south. When the Somali state collapsed 20 years ago, according to

1

Lewis, the "general tendency was for every major Somali clan to form its own militia movement."[3] People grouped themselves according to clan lines to seek protection amidst a widespread anarchy.

With the demise of the Somali state, the clan became once again an important factor of social grouping but also a societal factor contributing to bloody rivalries and fierce competition for power and resources, as Lewis mentioned: "Thus clans were becoming effectively self-governing entities throughout the Somali region as they carved out spheres of influence in a process which, with the abundance of modern weapons, frequently entailed savage battles with a high toll of civilian casualties."[4]

In the northern part of the country the population succeeded in establishing peace and reconciliation in a traditional way. This peace process led to the formation of two autonomous regions; namely Somaliland and Puntland. The South did not follow a similar path and continuous rivalry and fierce clashes between warlords turned the southern part of the country into total chaos. It is in an environment characterized by anarchy that the Islamic movements emerged with a powerful uniting message as an alternative to the warlord faction leaders.

### Renewed International efforts.

During the last decade, the international community has renewed its efforts to stabilize the country by supporting the reconstitution of Somali political institutions. A first attempt to find a political solution generated a Transitional National Government (TNG) after a reconciliation conference held in Arta, Djibouti in 2000. But according to Afyare Abdi Elmi, most of the warlords did not participate in the talks and Ethiopia, which backed some of them, "rejected the outcome, arguing that the Arta peace process

2

was incomplete."[5] This opposition to TNG efforts was detrimental and impeded it from imposing its control on Mogadishu and other areas of Somalia. Another row of reconciliation conferences were held in Mbaghati, in Kenya and after two years of deliberation a Transitional Federal Government was established (TFG), headed by Abdullahi Youssouf, in 2004. This TFG, although receiving much more support than the previous one could never achieve a wide reconciliation process or move into Mogadishu. Moreover, in 2006, with the support of the Ethiopian forces, it went to war with the Union of Islamic Court (UIC),[6] an umbrella group of Islamic movements who succeeded in controlling Mogadishu after defeating the various warlords.

The Ethiopian army defeated the UIC forces in December 2006, and the TFG was able to settle in Mogadishu. Shortly after these events an insurgency campaign started which made it difficult for the TFG and its Ethiopian ally to capitalize on their military gains. The former military wing of the UIC, the Alshabab (youths), the main forces of the new insurgency, gained popularity as a resistance movement.[7] Furthermore, as mentioned by Meredith Preston McGuie, some members of the TFG parliament defected and joined with the former leadership of the UIC as well as members of the Somali diaspora in an opposition movement; the Alliance for the Re-liberation of Somalia (ARS).[8] As pointed out by McGuie the "deterioration of the situation" and "the political deadlock" induced the need for a political solution.[9] According to her, "amid increasing calls for a political solution to the crisis a number of external actors begun to make discreet moves to try to build a constituency for political dialogue between these two groups."[10]

In 2008, an effort at mediation was launched by Djibouti with the support of the United Nations (UN). One year later, on February 2009, the Djibouti Peace Process engendered a new Transitional Federal Government (TFG) with the inclusion of members of the opposition who were part of the Union of the Islamic Court.[11] The former executive leader of the Union of the Islamic Court was now the new president of the TFG and sharia law is the law of the Somali state alongside a secular charter which regulates the TFG transitional institutions. Despite all these developments the civil war did not cease in Somalia, mainly because the main insurgent group, Alshabab, refused to participate in the peace process rejecting any talks or any agreements not calling for the departure of foreign troops from Somalia, including the African Union forces.

## The African Union Mission for Somalia

The presence of African Union troops is one of the major points of contention. In February 2007, the UN Security Council resolution 1744 authorized the deployment of African Union forces in Somalia; the African Union Mission in Somalia (AMISOM).[12] Article IV of the Status of Mission Agreement (SOMA)[13] between the Transitional Federal Government of the Somali Republic and the African Union on the African Union Mission in Somalia (AMISOM), signed in March 2007, expresses the mandate of the mission, and in paragraph 6, the size of the forces and its different components are laid out: "In this respect, the deployment of AMISOM, consisting of 9 infantry battalions, police and Civilian components, supported by Maritime and air elements was authorized. The mission element shall be drawn from AU Member States and shall number between 8,000 and 9,000 personnel (civilians inclusive)." Initially their mandate was for six months only, but due to the security situation, which did not improve, the mission was extended several times. Currently, Uganda and Burundi are the main contributors of the

AMISOM forces and Djibouti announced in March 2011 that it will contribute by sending two battalions to Somalia.[14]

The latest extension of the AMISOM mandate was in December 2010, which prolonged the African Union forces presence until September 2011.[15] Besides the presence of AMISOM forces there are other points of confrontation which can be categorized as political and doctrinal.

The rise of fundamentalist Islamism in Somalia is really striking, because this country was known for its lawlessness and its warlords. According to Bruton "the shabaab militia started to gain popular backing as a resistance movement."[16]The Islamic insurgency in its struggle for power in Somalia made an allegiance with Al-Qaida and undertakes suicide bombings and terror tactics previously unheard of in Somali history.

Currently, the TFG supported by a 9,000 strong African Union Forces controls the major parts of the capital, Mogadishu. On the other hand, Alshabab continues to hold the southern and central parts of Somalia, showing that they can transcend clan-divisions and obtain support from at least some segments of the Somali population. According to Bruton "before capturing a territory, the Shabaab typically engages in an extensive public relations effort, featuring public rallies and radio announcements, and ending in a voluntary reception of Shabaab leaders by clan elders, who retain significant power."[17] Besides the military aspect, a doctrinal confrontation in Islamic interpretation is taking place in Somalia between moderates in the Transitional Federal Government (TFG) and the traditionalist Sufis on one side, and Alshabab movement on the other side.

## Islamic movements in Somalia

Historically, Islam has been part of Somalis environment for centuries. Islam came into the Horn of Africa in the 7th century when a group of Muslims fleeing persecution conducted by the ruling tribe in Mecca, immigrated into Abyssinia.[18] According to Elmi, Somali oral history recounts the arrival of Muslim emigrants in Zeila a northern port town at the time of prophet Mohamed.[19] However Lewis mentioned that the conversion of Somalis is dated to around the 9th and 10th centuries.[20] The earlier Islamic movements known as *Tariqa*, (ways), were dedicated to spreading the teachings of Islam. Over time they became part of Somali culture and they exist today as peaceful and apolitical congregations. According to Lewis a more politically oriented movement is the one launched in the beginning of the 20th century by Sayyid Abdullah Hassan.[21] Sayyid Abdullah called for jihad against Britain and Italy and their colonial control before being defeated in 1920.

After Somalia achieved independence, the Islamic movements still existed but they had no political agenda. It is only after the military coup by Barre and the revolution launched by his military regime that a gulf began to appear between ruling elites and the different Islamic movements. When the Barre government promulgated a new family law, this reform was met with a large opposition by the religious leaders who publicly expressed their dissentions. The government response was a brutal repression of the law's opposition which culminated in the jailing and execution of 10 *Ulema* (religious leaders) in 1975.[22] The following years were characterized by oppression and tyranny under the iron grip of Siad Barre and his security apparatus. No room was left for opposing views, whether secular or religious.

Although the roots of the current Somali Islamism can be retraced in the past, the nature of the Alshabab movement as well as their message is very different from any previous religious movement in Somalia. The revival of Islamic militancy can be linked with the fall of Barre's dictatorial regime and the disintegration of the Somali state.[23] It is only in the last twenty years that the Islamic militancy became very active in Somalia, in various forms, political and apolitical, moderate and radical.

However, beside the brief emergence of Alittihad, the earliest Islamic movement with a political agenda in Somalia, in what is currently known as the Puntland region, no Islamist movement has ever settled a durable footprint or achieved control over wide regions in the north of the country.[24] One of the main reasons is that the populations of those northern regions have largely resolved their issues and established fully functioning secular institutions in Somaliland and in Puntland. The failure of the southern leadership has impeded a similar conflict resolution process in the South.

This failure has created the conditions for Islamic militant groups to present themselves as an alternative to the warlords and other faction-leaders. It has been a gradual process which has helped restore some sort of normality and security to the population in the south. Since 2006 even these Islamic groups have become divided on various issues and their dialectic has turned violent as when Alshabab refused to take part in the peace conference held in Djibouti in 2009.

The clash and then merger between Alshabab and Hizbull Islam,[25] in December of 2010 is the latest example of Alshabab's unwillingness for political plurality. The former leader of Hizbul Islam; Daher Aweys is now a member of Alshabab. Whether he has a key function in the movement is not clear and unlikely. What are also unclear are

Alshabab's ultimate objectives and vision for Somalia. Their ban on the national Somali flag is an indication of a transnational agenda but there is some sign that this particular agenda is not well shared by all members who aspire for a more nationally oriented strategy. According to Bruton, Daher Aweys is perceived to have a more nationally oriented agenda as he has publicly criticized, in the past, Al Qaida interference in Somalia.[26] It seems that the core leadership of Alshabab do not all has the same approach. How this important question will be solved by the movement is unknown, but the recent offensive launched by the government and its allies such as Ahlu Suna Wal Jama'a[27] (ASWJ) and Ras Kamboni groups has shaken Alshabab's grip on southern Somalia. There are indications that the Islamic movement is trying to obtain the support of the people. How are they going to gain support of the population with an everlasting jihadist agenda? How could refusing any political negotiations or power sharing bring peace?

## Thesis Question

The purpose of this study is to understand the emergence of Alshabab, the Islamic insurgency in Somalia. This question centers on the genesis of the group, their strategic mistakes and their evolution. The thesis question is how Alshabab has emerged in Somalia?

The subordinate question to this thesis concerns the adequacy of the current predominant militaristic approach against the radical group. Is defeating Alshabab the only way for peace in Somalia?

## Assumptions

The current political stalemate is unlikely to be solved any time soon unless both parties agree on a comprehensive conflict resolution process. Due to its absolutist logic Alshabab has not been able to capitalize on its success such as establishing security and presenting itself as a major political player. Moreover their willingness to use terrorism as political means has made them anathema in the region and throughout the world. Its opponents are not praiseworthy either; according to an International Crisis Group report[28] published in February 2011, the TFG is plagued by internal dysfunction and corruption which impede the extension of its control in areas outside Mogadishu.

## Limitations

Analysis will be restricted to those areas in Somalia where Islamic principles were used as a mode of governance, namely the South and Central Somalia. It is only in these areas that the Islamic militancy has been able to gain influence and control. This is due to the fact that unlike their southern counterparts the northern leadership has been able to settle a reconciliation process which led to the creation of two autonomous regions; Somaliland and Puntland. The relative peace and security existing in these regions have not favored the rise of Islamic militancy and radical elements aiming at gaining power.

The rise of Islamic militancy in Somalia is a relatively new phenomenon and the literature on the subject is still inchoate. The situation there has evolved, with the emergence of a more radical movement, Alshabab, who has made an allegiance to Al-Qaida, and who is willing to use terrorism to achieve its goal.[29] Finally, access to current developments in Somalia will be limited to open sources.

## Conclusion

In Somalia the lack of a strong, legitimate, legal and coercive central power has

compelled the population to seek protection from their clan, thus perpetuating the

existence of faction leaders and warlords. These warlords are more interested in their own

mercantile and illegal activities than the reconstruction of the Somali state. Any prospects

of building government institutions are continuously met with difficulties. In the North

more traditional ways have led to reconciliation and functioning secular institutions. In

southern Somalia Islamist groups seem to have found some solutions in how to overcome

the warlords and ensure security. However their unwillingness to compromise have

become a challenge which the TFG will to have to address, one way or another, for a

long lasting peace in Somalia. This research is focused on grasping the nature of the

Somali Islamism; more particularly, the examination will be focused on Alshabab and its

goals.

---

[1]Terrence Lyons and Ahmed I. Samatar, *Somalia: State Collapse, Multilateral Intervention, and Strategies for Political Reconstruction* (Washington, DC: Brookings Occasional Papers, 1995), 14.

[2]An Africa Watch Report, *Somalia: A Government at war with its own people. Testimonies about the Killings and the Conflict in the North* (United States of America: The Africa Watch Committee, 1990), 44.

[3]Ioan. M. Lewis, *Blood and Bone: The Call of Kinship in Somali Society* (Lawrenceville, NJ: The Red Sea Press, 1994), 231.

[4]Ibid.

[5]Afyare Abdi Elmi, *Understanding The Somalia Conflagration: Identity, Political Islam and Peacebuilding* (London: Pluto Press, 2010), 99.

[6]Ibid., 84.

[7]Bronwyn E. Bruton, *Somalia: A New Approach* (United States of America: Council on Foreign Relations, 2010), 8.

[8]Meredith Preston McGuie, "Mediating Djibouti," Conciliation Resources, 2010, http://www.c-r.org/our-work/accord/somalia/mediating-djibouti.php (accessed June 11, 2011).

[9]Ibid.

[10]Ibid.

[11]Ibid.

[12]Security Council, SC/8960, "Security Council Authorizes Six-Month African Union Mission in Somalia." United Nations, Department of Public Information News and Media Division, February 20, 2007, http://www.un.org/News/Press/docs/2007/ sc8960.doc.htm (accessed June 15, 2011).

[13]African Union Mission in Somalia (AMISOM), http://www.africa-union.org/root/AU/AUC/Departments/PSC/AMISOM/amisom.htm (accessed 28 June, 2011).

[14]Voice of America, "Djibouti to soon send Peacekeepers to Somalia," May 14, 2011, http://blogs.voanews.com/breaking-news/2011/05/14/djibouti-to-soon-send-peacekeepers-to-somalia (accessed June 30, 2011).

[15]Security Council, SC/10139, "Security Council extends authorization of African Union Mission in Somalia until 30 September 2011," December 22, 2010, http://www.un.org/News/Press/docs/2010/sc10139.doc.htm (accessed June 15, 2011).

[16]Bruton, 8.

[17]Ibid., 11.

[18]International Board of Islamic Research and Resources, "The First Hijra: Migration to Abyssinia," http: //www.ethiopolitics.com/articles/The_first_hijra.htm, (accessed June 11, 2011).

[19]Elmi, 49.

[20]I. M. Lewis, *Saints and Somalis: Popular Islam in a Clan-Based Society*, (Lawrenceville, NJ: Red Sea Press, 1998), 7.

[21]Ibid., 69.

[22]Elmi, 57.

[23]Shaul Shay, *Somalia between Jihad and Restoration* (New Brunswick, NJ: Translation Publishers, 2008), 37.

[24]A. Duale Siiarag, "The Birth and Rise of Al-Ittihad Al-Islami in the Somali inhabited Regions in The Horn of Africa," Waardheernews.com, November 13, 2005, http://wardheernews-com/articles/November/13_Alittihad_sii%27arag.html (accessed May 24, 2011).

[25]BBC News, "Somali Islamists Al-shabab and Hizbul Islam 'to merge,'" December 20, 2010, http://www.bbc.co.uk/news/world-africa-12038556 (accessed May 24, 2011).

[26]Bruton, 10.

[27]Ibid., 11.

[28]International Crisis Group, Africa Report no. 170, "Somalia: The Transitional Government on Life Support," February 21, 2011, http://www.crisisgroup.org/en/regions/africa/horn-of-africa/somalia/170-somalia-the-transitional-government-on-life-support.aspx (accessed June 30, 2011).

[29]Bruton, 16.

CHAPTER 2

LITERATURE REVIEW

Alshabab has become a major actor in Somalia despite the recent efforts by the

Transitional government supported by the international community to counter this

movement. In order to analyze its strategy it is important to understand its doctrine and

the context in which this global jihadist movement has emerged. This chapter will

explore the literature concerning the Somalia civil war and the Islamic militancy which

appeared in part of the country. It is clearly noticeable that in general, the books and

articles written on the Islamic militancy in Somalia reflect the lack of visibility of these

movements in the early years following the fall of the Somalia dictatorial government.

Little has been written on the Islamic militancy in Somalia prior to the year 2000

for two reasons. First, these movements were not militarily active in the capital such as is

the case today. In the first half of the 1990s the spotlights were focused on the bloody

clan-based fights between warlords and the ensuing widespread humanitarian disaster and

famine. Secondly, the terrorist attacks on September 9, 2001 and the onward war on

terror launched by the Bush administration focused the attention of the international

community on the possibility of an Al-Qaida safe haven in Somalia.[1]

Some evidence attests that Islamic militant groups have been active since the

collapse of the state. They have had various goals; both apolitical and political, and they

sometimes clashed with other secular clan-based factions. One of the earliest Islamic

groups with a political agenda is Al ittihad al Islami, and authors such Menkhaus have

analyzed its development.[2] If authors have similar recount on the emergence of Islamic

militancy in Somalia, they diverge on the appropriate approach necessary to deal with this militancy. This chapter is organized thematically. First we will examine what authors have written about the collapse of the Somali state. Then we will explore the revival of Islamic militancy and the jihadist trend. Finally we will scrutinize the available information concerning Alshabab.

Somalia: A collapsed state

The demise of Barre's regime and the subsequent civil war destroyed Somalia as a unique political entity. The lack of a central power engulfed the country in years of anarchy and a disastrous humanitarian crisis. This collapse resulted from the degradation of the socio-political environment under Barre's regime. In their Book; *Somalia*, Terrence Lyons and Ahmed I. Samatar describe the process of State Collapse: "State collapse occurs when structure, authority, legitimate power, law, and political order fall apart, leaving behind a civil society that lacks the ability to rebound to fill the vacuum."[3]

After the fall of the government; according to Terrance and Samatar, Somalia became a Hobbesian world.[4] A world in which the boundary of what is right or wrong, just and unjust has been erased with the demise of the state. It is a condition described by Hobbes in his influential *Leviathan* in the following terms: "To this warre of every man against every man, this also is consequent; that nothing can be Unjust. The notions of Right and Wrong, Justice and Injustice have there no place. Where there is no common Power, there is no law: where no law, no injustice."[5]

In fact when Siad Barre fled his presidential palace, on January 27, 1991, under the pressure of a military insurgency coupled with a popular uprising, all the public structures designed to provide collective service and security literally disintegrated. The main reason of the anarchy in the Somali South is that the victorious insurgent movements such as Union of Somali Congress, (USC) and Somali Patriotic Movement (SPM) have failed to agree on one common leadership.[6] Furthermore, these different armed movements themselves became divided by internal feud.

The head of the military wing of the USC; Aided, which took the capital Mogadishu, saw himself as the obvious successor of the vanquished president. However another faction of USC composed of the Abgal clan, which are predominant in Mogadishu and the territory surrounding the capital, were reluctant to give the power to a military man fearing it might lead to another dictatorial rule (Aided was a former general). Therefore, they designated a business man named Ali Mahdi as a head of USC and as an interim president for Somalia.[7] This unilateral decision, led to more bloodshed and a fierce civil war which destroyed the entire infrastructure of the country, and tearing the Somali society apart.

An unparalleled level of violence based on clan rivalry engulfed the country in a total chaos. According to Lyons and Samatar, this unfortunate situation was the direct result of the ill-fated policies intentionally conducted by Said Barre for nearly two decades.[8] These policies caused the deterioration of the social cohesion which is the basis of the state: "The demise of a state is inherently linked to a breakdown of social coherence on an extensive level as civil society can no longer create, aggregate, and articulate the supports and demands that are the foundations of the state. Without the state, society breaks down and without social structures, the state cannot survive."[9]

Somali society is organized in clan structure, and naturally after the collapse of the state, the clan remained the only social structure left in which some protection and survival could be ensured. The warlords took advantage of the situation with a predatory

15

agenda in a deadly competition for resources. According to Gerard Prunier, these warlords had no legitimacy, but they have succeeded in a "decaying territorial and political context."[10] He criticizes the fact that despite their lack of legitimacy the international community gave them a predominant role in any reconciliation attempt which then caused the failure of these attempts.

This outcome was challenged by Islamic militant groups who arose amid the anarchy and strived to establish the rule of law on which every Somali clan could agree on; it being the sharia law and the Islamic principles. These Somali Islamic militant groups advocated the establishment of an Islamic state in Somalia. Their ideology and their trans-clannish message had an inherent centripetal force which assured them success against warlords in the South of Somalia. However, as these Islamic groups would later diverge, a more radical element appeared in Somalia.

## The Islamic militancy

In the Muslim world the emergence of Islamic militancy could be dated from the eighteenth century. The current Islamic movement should been seen as a continuation and not as a new phenomenon as writer Alex de Waal citing Michael Gilsenan points out:

> Michael Gilsenan rightly cautions against the tendency, among Muslims and non-Muslims alike, to simplify and homogenize 'Islam' (1982:18-19). He also reminds us that for two centuries (at least), there has been an ongoing process of Islamic 'revival,' so that contemporary Islamic militancy should not be seen as a wholly new phenomenon but rather as a continuation of an established tradition of renewal.[11]

This revival has taken two forms; one is a reaction against colonial power such as the Mahdist movement in Sudan and the other is a reformist movement aimed at changing

16

the society and the religious practices such as the Wahhabist movement in the Arabia peninsula.

The Mahdist movement was a resistance movement against the British conquest of Sudan. Alex de Waal notes that this movement has been seen and mythologized as a "revolutionary protonationalism."[12] The same could be said of the Sayyid Abdallah Hassan movement in Somalia in the beginning of the twentieth century. Despite his controversial legacy, Sayyid Abdullah is seen as the icon of Somali nationalism. These two movements in Sudan and in Somalia had some features in common. Both of them were a "Sufi-inspired jihadism, based upon the mystical vision of a charismatic leader."[13] However, these Islamic movements who resisted against a colonial power were both defeated militarily and ideologically. The nationalist movement of the twentieth century in their struggle for independence adopted and promoted a secular view of politics.

The other form of this revival is symbolized by the Wahhabi who succeeded in controlling much of the Arabian Peninsula (actual Saudi Arabia). The Wahhabi was a puritanical reformist movement which promoted a strict adherence to Islamic principles and emulation of the first generations of Muslims, the Salaf.[14] Many of the actual Islamic militant groups bear the same message.

In the twentieth century several authors are widely acknowledged for their thoughts on Political Islam and their influential writings. One is Hassan Albanna who is the founder of the Muslim Brotherhood movement. This movement emerged in Egypt in 1928 and after decades of turbulent relationships with the various secular Egyptian governments, it is currently a major player in the political scene due to its rejection of violence. Another contributor to the Islamic militancy is Sayyid Qutb who was sentenced to death by Nasser regime and executed in 1966. Sayyid Qutb's book, *Milestones*, influenced many of the current leaders of the Islamic militancy. His writings are the main reference of the global jihadist movement such as Al-Qaida who advocate Qutb's principles and rejection of what he has called "Jahiliya"; by this word Qutb characterized the modern civilization and the cultural dominance of the West as decadent.[15]

Although Al Banna and Qutb were both Arabs and Egyptian, others scholars from the Muslim world contributed to the development of Islamic thought. Mawdudi, from Pakistan, was a prolific author and a fervent advocate of what could be called the "islamisation of the political scene." Mawdudi promoted the integration between religion and politics, and called for a revolution in leadership. According to him this revolution has a central place in Islam.[16] Moreover, he claims that a political leadership devoted to lead according to the Islamic principles is a necessary condition in order to fulfill individually and collectively God prescriptions:

> The objective of the Islamic movement, in this world, is revolution in leadership. A leadership that has rebelled against God and His guidance and is responsible for the suffering of mankind has to be replaced by a leadership that is God-conscious, righteous and committed to following Divine guidance. Striving to achieve this noble purpose, we believe, will secure God's favor in this world and in the next.[17]

Mawdudi's call for revolution in leadership was facilitated in Somalia by the demise of the government. The power vacuum created and the subsequent anarchy set the conditions for the emergence of Islamic movements with the aim of establishing an Islamic state in Somalia.

## Islamic militancy in Somalia

Until the US led peacekeeping mission in 1992, little is known about the various militant groups in Somalia. In fact Aided, the warlord in control Mogadishu, warned the

18

US led coalition against hostile actions from fundamentalist groups whom they saw as rivals. Aided even asked the US forces for a coordinated military operation against a fundamentalist group called Somali National Islamic Front (SNIF).[18] Shawn Shay in his book *Somalia between jihad and restoration* (2008) has identified three categories[19] of Islamic movements in Somalia: political Islamism, missionary Islamism, and jihadi Islamism.

He acknowledges the difference in this militancy and he warns against the empowerment of the radical element in Somalia. He calls for an "alternative to the Islamic model," by supporting a secular government.[20] The problem is that people saw that this model could bring them stability and security as was the case in 2006 before the Ethiopian invasion brutally ended the rule of the UIC (Union of Islamic Court). Basically he advocates a proactive approach and the deployment of an international force to "help the government fight its opponents."[21]

Bronwyn Bruton has a different view. In a study published in 2010 by the Council on Foreign Affairs, an independent research institute, she proposes a more pragmatic approach which seeks conformity with the reality on the ground. Although Bruton recognizes that Al-Qaida elements must be targeted in Somalia she advices restraint and the avoidance of collateral damage to the population. She proposes a "constructive disengagement" in order to "encourage disaggregation of radical movements by adopting a position of neutrality."[22] The aim of this approach is to reach the more nationalistic leader such as Daher Aweys and to isolate the radical element within the movement and undermine their influence by showing a "willingness to coexist with any Islamism authority" provided that this authority reject any global jihadist agenda.[23]

## Al- Ittihad legacy: The Rise of Sharia courts

Years before Bruton, Menkhaus warned in an article published in 2003 against any "boilerplate approach" which ignores the differences between the Islamic groups in Somalia.[24] Historically Al-Ittihad Al-Islami is the first movement with a political agenda who entered in a competition with the warlords in the first half of the 1990s. Menkhaus described this group as a movement dedicated to restore order by implementing sharia law in the context of a collapsed state embroiled in anarchy. He also noted that this group was not unified in a common vision. Its members departed on the strategy and the goals they should pursue. It is the main reason why this group has been militarily defeated by Ethiopian forces and some clan based factions. For Menkhaus all the members of Alittihad did not share the same global jihadist doctrine.

This point of view is not shared by Duale who is less complacent and describes them as a "shadow force" still operating under the radar in Somalia despite the fact that Alittihad no longer exists as an organization.[25] Despite its failure of controlling a wide region Alittihad left an important legacy in Somalia; the use of Islamic principles as system of government and the rule of law.

According to Menkhaus the need for a secure environment was raised by the business community who gradually withdrew its support from the warlords who have failed on this matter even in the territory under their control.[26] The Sharia courts were created to provide justice and security in face of the lack of government and the rule of law. These sharia courts were collaborating with the warlords as they were clan-based and they restricted themselves only to judicial matters. They even accepted to dismiss their troops after the formation of the first TFG (transitional federal government) in 2000

20

in Arta; Djibouti. However, the situation deteriorated gradually as the TFG could not extend its control outside Mogadishu and the warlords were reluctant to be stripped of their power. Meanwhile the war on terror was launched and United States stepped up its effort to mitigate any possible Al-Qaida attempt to use Somalia as a rear base. The US was also on the hunt for members of al-Qaida linked with the bloody attack on the American embassy in Kenya and Tanzania in 1998.

A US supported Alliance for Restoration of Peace and Counterterrorism (ARPCT) emerged suddenly in the Somali political scene in 2005.[27] It was nothing less than an opportunistic association of the main warlords who saw this as a way to make political and financial gain. According to Bruton, this new organization had a negative impact on the Somali society.[28] Elmi also mentioned that the Islamists were revolted against the numerous arrests of individuals and religious scholars that the warlords were conducting.[29]

All the sharia courts then unified under the name of Union of Islamic Court (UIC) and with the support of the population clashed militarily with the ARPCT and defeated them. In a few weeks Mogadishu was cleared from any ARPCT supported warlords. The Union of Islamic Courts proceeded to disarm the clan based factions and they removed all the checkpoints which have divided the city for fifteen years.[30] The UIC despite its success, such as reopening the port and the airport closed for more than a decade and restoring security, was unable to reach an accord on power sharing with the TFG. It was also struggling against a negative perception held by the international community who saw them as a radical group.

Ethiopia also saw the UIC and its success as a direct threat to its security. As a preemptive action and with the support of the TFG, Ethiopian forces invaded Somalia in December 2006. They rapidly overran the UIC military forces and took the capital city deserted by the defeated UIC forces. It is these events which triggered the wider radicalization process and the call for jihad in Somalia. Alshabab, a military wing of the UIC, become the symbol of national resistance when it started an insurgency campaign which is still underway today.

## The Emergence of Alshabab

The literature concerning Alshabab is limited. This is due to the fact that the emergence of this group is a new phenomenon in Somalia. Of particular relevance is the recent book of Afyare A.Elmi, *Understanding the Somalia Conflagration: Political Islam and Peace building*, (2010) and the studies conducted in the same year by Bronwyn E. Bruton.

A more recent study was published in March 2011 by Roland Marchal, a researcher in the French Center for Scientific Research.[31] There are many articles written on the recent political developments in Somalia and the impact of the Alshabab movement. The movement itself has released a number of materials composed of audio messages and video footages of combat scenes in Mogadishu. There are also some websites, such as www.somalimemo.com, which support the group and who release updated news on the recent activity of the group. Their informational messaging is confronted with ones from other websites, such as www.radiomogadishu.com, neutral or opposed to the Alshabab allowing depictions of a less blurred picture of this movement.

The key issue in the current conflict is the rejection by Alshabab of the UN sponsored African Union troop presence in Somalia. They consider their presence as a continuation of the foreign occupation and the denial by the international community of the establishment of an Islamic state in Somalia.[32] As mentioned by Bruton, Alshabab has embraced the global jihad ideology and made a "formal declaration of allegiance to Al-Qaida on February 2, 2010."[33]

This group has welcomed foreign fighters who believe in the call for Jihad promoted by Al Qaida. Its leader who bears the title of Amir is Ahmad Abdi Godane also known as Sheikh Abu Zuber. In a recent broadcast on radio Mogadishu[34] Godane's biography was retraced, he was depicted as having been trained in Afghanistan where he made frequent travels while studying in Pakistan.

It appears that the movement is well organized with a political bureau that seems in charge of the administration and public relations. There is also a military wing and a security force, and units or cells in charge of suicide attacks. The main peculiarity of this movement is that it continues to provide humanitarian relief to the population under their control while fighting against the governmental forces and AMISOM. Their willingness to use terrorism has closed all doors for talks between them and the actual TFG and both parties are locked in the logic of war.[35]

## Conclusion

Although the literature on the topic is limited, the existing writings and number of web based materials permit an analysis of the emergence of the Islamic militancy in Somalia. The Alshabab phenomenon will no doubt inspire in the years to come more literature than available today because the impact of the current events in Somalia is affecting the whole region. The collapse of the Somali state has caused the disintegration of all public structures and the institutional framework inherited from the colonial era. After a decade of an unfruitful democracy and parliamentary regime, Siad Barre's military power imposed a "scientique socialism" not suited for the social and cultural reality. When confronted with criticism Barre engineered a divisive and dangerous clan policy destined to ensure power for him and its close circle. The events of the last two decades of anarchy are the direct result of this ill-fated policy.

The Islamic militancy has emerged in the context of a collapsed state, and its aim was to establish primarily security and the rule of law. The more politically oriented Islamic movement Al-ittihad, failed to establish an Islamic state because Somalis were in the midst of a clan war fueled by rivalries and competition between warlords. Their legacy consisted primarily of the numerous sharia courts who gained popularity in late 1990s, helped gradually establish the rule of law in the chaotic environment of Central and South Somalia. It was the rule of law based on Islamic principles which instilled a relative normality. As recognized by authors such as Elmi and Bruton, it also favored the emergence of a radical element that became empowered by the Ethiopian invasion in 2006.

Alshabab is currently fighting to impose their ideology based on sharia and jihad. The form of a political system based on Islamic principles outlined in the Koran and the Hadiths is open to discussion according to Muslim scholars such as Mohammad Hashim Kamali.[36] The latter claims that Islam promotes political pluralism and not authoritarianism. In Somalia, an important factor of the political stalemate is that Alshabab has made allegiance to Al-*Qaida,* and it has embraced the global jihad ideology. Furthermore they have emulated the same methods such as terrorism and

suicide attack. Therefore any prospect of political discussions became very difficult.

Balancing the nationalist agenda with a focus on Somalia and the global jihad is the main

challenge of Alshabab in its struggle to gain power.

---

[1]Bruton, 6.

[2]Kenneth J. Menkhaus, "Political Islam in Somalia," http://www.somali-jna.org/downloads/Menkhaus%20-%20Political%20Islam%20in%20Somalia.pdf (accessed April 20, 2011).

[3]Lyons and Samatar, 1.

[4]Ibid., 7.

[5]Thomas Hobbes, *Leviathan* (Mineola, NY: Dover Publications, Inc, 2006), 71.

[6]Lyons and Samatar, 22.

[7]Ibid.

[8]Ibid., 24.

[9]Ibid., 1.

[10]Gerard Prunier, chercheur au CNRS, directeur du Centre Francais des Etudes Ethiopiennes (Addis Abeba) [Head of the French Center for the Ethiopian Studies (Addis Abeba)], Propos recueillis par Robert Wiren [Interviewed by Robert Wiren], *Les Nouvelles D'Addis* [Addis News], http://www.lesnouvelles.org/P10_magazine/15_grandentretien/15013_gerardprunier.html (accessed June 19, 2011).

[11]Alex De Waal ed., *Islamism and Its Enemies in the Horn of Africa* (Bloomington, IN: Indiana University Press, 2004), 2.

[12]Ibid., 4.

[13]Ibid.

[14]Ibid.

[15]Seyyid Qutb, *Milestones* (Damascus, Syria: Dar Al-Ilm, n.d), 11.

[16]Sayyid Abul A'la Mawdudi, *The Islamic Movement: Dynamics of Values, Power, and Change*, ed. Khurram Murad (Leicester, UK: The Islamic Foundation, 1998), 71.

[17]Ibid.

[18]Robert F. Baumann and Lawrence A. Yates with Versalle F. Washington, *My Clan Against the World, US and Coalition Forces in Somalia, 1992-1994* (Fort Leavenworth, KS: Combat Studies Institute Press, 2004), 42.

[19]Shaul Shay, *Somalia between Jihad and Restoration* (New Brunswick, NJ: Transaction Publishers, 2008), 38.

[20]Ibid., 195.

[21]Ibid., 197.

[22]Bruton, 26.

[23]Ibid.

[24]Menkhaus, 122.

[25]Duale.

[26]Menkhaus, 116.

[27]Bruton, 7.

[28]Ibid.

[29]Afyare Abdi Elmi, *Understanding The Somalia Conflagration: Identity, Political Islam and Peacebuilding* (London: Pluto Press, 2010), 83.

[30]Ibid.

[31]Roland Marchal, "The Rise of A jihadi Movement in a Country at War: Harakat Al-Shabaab Al Mujaheddin in Somalia," http://www.ceri-sciences-po.org/ressource/shabaab.pdf (accessed July 2011), 4.

[32]Daveed Gartenstein-Ross and Seungwon Chung, "The African Union's beleaguered Somalia Mission," *The Long War Journal*, July 20, 2010, http://www.long warjournal.org/archiv (accessed May 17, 2011).

[33]Bruton, 16.

[34]Radiomogadisho, "Taariikhda Axmed Godane" [Biographie of Ahmed Godane], radiomogadisho, May 12, 2011, http://radiomuqdisho.net/taariikhda-axmed-godane-dhagayso/ (accessed May 25, 2011).

[35]Bill Roggio, "Shabaab claims credit for dual suicide attacks in Uganda," *The Long War Journal*, July 12, 2010, http://www.longwarjournal.org/archiv (accessed May 17, 2011).

[36]Mohammad Hashim Kamali, *Shari`ah Law: An Introduction* (Oxford, UK: Oneworld Publication, 2008), 202.

# CHAPTER 3

## RESEARCH METHODOLOGY

This thesis will be a qualitative research study using the narrative research method. Catherine Marshall and Gretchen B.Rossman assert that "qualitative studies typically focus on individuals, dyads, groups, processes, or organizations."[1] The narrative research method emphasizes the contextualization of stories and their chronology. This is particularly suitable for this study, which aims to understand the emergence of Alshabab in Somalia.

Referring to Czarniawska, John W. Creswell defines narrative as "a specific type of qualitative design in which narrative is understood as a spoken or written text giving an account of an event/action or series of events/actions, chronologically connected."[2] He proposes a four steps procedure for conducting a narrative research. The first step is to "determine if the research problem or question best fit narrative research."[3] He adds that "narrative research is best for capturing the detailed stories or life experiences of a single life or the lives of a small number of individuals."[4] The second step is to "select one or more individuals who have stories or life experiences to tell, and spend considerable time with them gathering their stories through multiples types of information."[5] The third step of the procedure is to "collect information about the context of these stories."[6] Here the chronological aspect and the historical context are also included. The fourth step is the analysis. Creswell describes this step as "restorying," which "is the process of reorganizing the stories into some general type of framework."[7] In this latter process, the researcher "provides a causal link among ideas."[8]

28

The analysis will be conducted by examining a number of themes. These themes will help understand the historical context in which Alshabab emerged. This approach is conforming to what Creswell described as an analysis using "multiple levels of abstraction."[9] Creswell asserts that "often, writers present their studies in stages (e.g., the multiple themes that can be combined into larger themes or perspectives) or layer their analyses from the particular to the general. The codes and themes derived from the data might show mundane, expected, and surprising ideas."[10] A similar approach will be employed for this research.

Finally, Creswell asserts that the narrative method implies the development of a relationship between the participants and the researcher.[11] Obviously, the latter proposition is difficult to achieve for this research due to the nature of the topic. Conducting research on a radical organization and gaining insight of their movement is never an easy task. The challenge for this study is more an epistemological question than anything else. How do we know what we know? The main constraint being that, in this research, there are no empirical observations in the field. However, this constraint is leveled by thoroughly reviewing the literature on the subject, and a daily review of the Somali and international media news. Additionally, the various views of scholars who studied Somalia predicament are taken in consideration.

Fortunately, as Creswell mentioned, narrative research is not a "lock-step approach."[12] Therefore for the purpose of this research, the first step of the adopted methodology is to describe the topic, its importance, and how it fits the narrative method. The second step is to assert how the data collected will be used and analyzed in order to answer the first and second thesis questions. Finally, the last step of this methodology is to describe the challenges of this method and the adequate measures which could assure the objectivity of this research.

<u>Defining the problem</u>

According to Torill Moen a "narrative is a story that tells a sequence of events that is significant for the narrator or her or his audience."[13] She also asserts that narratives "capture both the individual and the context."[14] This is what is intended for this research. The purpose of this study is to understand the emergence of Alshabab, the Islamic insurgency in Somalia. This radical movement is conducting an insurgency war against the Transitional Federal Government (TFG) formed in Djibouti in 2009 after a peace process between various Somalis factions. Besides refusing to participate in the peace process, Alshabab adopted the use of terrorist methods. Its allegiance with Al-Qaida has raised hurdles for any future prospect of negotiations between the Islamist movement and the TFG. Although it seems that Al-Qaida does not control the Somali Islamic insurgents, the available sources permit to assert that there are strong links between Alshabab and the global jihad network.[15]

The appearance of suicide bombing and other terrorist methods in Somalia is striking and deserves examination.[16] These methods are what distinguish Alshabab from the other armed groups in Somalia. Another characteristic of Alshabab is their uncompromising view on sharia law as unique rule of law and the commitment to jihad against foreign military presence in Somalia.[17] In Somali traditions, according to Lewis "the application of the Shariah tends to be restricted to intra-clan affairs and certain matters of personal status."[18] Lewis also stated that "even within the clan, the jurisdiction of the Shariah is limited by the force of local custom (heer, tastuur)."[19] The literature on the subject of the sharia by Islamic scholars offers a less rigid picture. Mohamed Hashim Kamali in his book, *Sharia law: An Introduction* (2008) argues that Islam promotes the concept of "Shura" (consultation) in the daily matters of the Muslim community and excludes any manly authoritarianism alongside the rule of God.[20] He also states that the Islamic principle of "Ikhtilaf" (disagreement) allow pluralism and divergence of opinion as long as the dogmatic principles of Islam such as the unicity of God are not in question.[21] Alshabab has a more strict interpretation of the Islamic principles, and their main doctrine is the jihad against foreign forces in Somalia.[22] The data collected for this research permits an analysis of the context and the chronological events that led to the emergence of this movement. This research explores the current insurgency in Somalia, conducted by Alshabab. This movement adheres to the bellicose global jihad ideology. It is the adherence to this ideology which poses a threat to the stability of the entire Horn of Africa.[23]

## Making sense of the Data collected

According to Creswell "narrative research has many forms, uses a variety of analytic practices, and is rooted in different social and humanities disciplines."[24] For this research the "narrative analysis"[25] approach will be employed. In narrative analysis, "researchers collect descriptions of events or happenings and then configure them into a story using a plot line."[26] Although the object of this research concerns the Somali terrorist organization, the analysis will not be conducted exclusively through the lens of counter-terrorism. As Menkhaus stated "consumers of analyses of the terrorist threat in Somalia must approach this topic with appropriate caution."[27] The ideas advanced by Afyare Abdi Elmi in his book *Undesrtanding Somalia Conflagration* (2010) are useful

31

for this research. He claims that identity redefinition is at the center of the Somali problem and he adheres to the theory of social constructivism and the assumption that "social realities are rooted in specific structures that can be changed."[28] This is particularly interesting for this research because the clan factor and power sharing is at the core of Somali problems, much more than the global jihadist ideology which only appeared recently.

In the context of the collapsed state Islamic movements appeared first with the intention of filling this vacuum in competition with the infamous warlords. In recent years the social structure of Somalis prevented any attempt to establish a central authority and a government with legitimate coercive power. The Islamic militancy found a way to transcend this hindrance and it is interesting to examine their methods. Elmi proposes also analyzing the Somalia case through "post-colonialism paradigms" and the need to understand the colonial legacy.[29] The collapse of the State and the failure of the post-independence leadership show that, in Somalia, institutions inherited from the colonial past were fragile because they were not rooted in an indigenous and genuine process which could have ensured a solid basis. Elmi also acknowledged there exists too often a negative perception of Islam in Western societies.[30] This perception of Islam as a threat to Occidental cultural values has been heightened by the emergence of Islamic militancy and particularly the global jihadist trend.

In this study the Somali civil war is seen first and foremost as an internal evolution of the Somali society in which the Islamic movement intend to participate. This participation has taken unfortunately violent ways. By doing so the cultural, traditional, and religious values are reshaped in a violent conflict. This violence inherent in all human societies could have had a less destructive scope in Somalia without external intervention such as the Ethiopian military invasion. We shall also include in these external factors impacting on the Somalia political situation the adherence by Alshabab to the global jihadist ideology and their allegiance to Al-Qaida which in return provided them with substantial support.[31]

In this research, although we share the same view mentioned by Afyare Abdi Elmi we found it also valuable to undertake this study by considering the Somali predicament as pertaining to the realm of Political Philosophy. The main concepts of Political Philosophy are helpful in order to grasp the socio-political evolution which is taking place in Somalia. For instance the writing of Hobbes and Rousseau[32] help understand the process of the constitution of a society and its system of governance. The concept of "common wealth"[33] is particularly interesting. Hobbes defined it as the process of men freely agreeing to erect a common power to preserve collectively their individual rights:

> This is more than Consent, or Concord; it is a reall Unitie of them all in one and the same Person, made by Covenant of every man with every man, in such manner, as if every man should say to every man, *I Authorise and give up my Right of Governing my selfe, to this Man, or to this Assembly of men, on this condition, that thou give up thy Right to him , and Authorise all his Actions in like manner*. This done, the Multitude so united in one Person, is called a COMMON-WEALTH, in latine CIVITAS.[34]

In Somalia, the Islamic militancy emerged first with the aim of resolving the anarchical situation and unifying Somalis. This anarchy was fueled by faction leaders and warlords who had also failed to unite Somalis, particularly in the South and Central Somalia. The Islamic militancy in general and Alshabab in particular are engaged in a process of transforming the Somali society by using religion as a unifying catalyst.

33

<u>Methodological Challenges</u>

Due to the inherent limitations of this topic, the research will be conducted exclusively through documentation and secondary sources. However, as recognized by Creswell, this methodology has also some challenges which need to be addressed.[35] He asserts that "the researcher needs to collect extensive information about the participant, and needs to have a clear understanding of the context of the individual's life."[36] Furthermore, he proposes the following steps for Data analysis and representation process: "Data managing, Describing, Classifying, Interpreting, Representing, and Visualizing." Following this process could ensure the objectivity of this research given the wide variety of information obtained.

The data used in this research was acquired by a thorough review of Somali literature. A significant amount of information was obtained from web based materials such as articles, news and internet blogs. Therefore, it is necessary to categorize this materiel. Data collection is a critical step. Creswell asserts that "the research question drive the data collection and analysis rather than the reverse being the case."[37] This research methodology adheres to this principle. To ensure the credibility of this research, the validation process described by Creswell will be used. Referring to Angel, Creswell asserts that validation is defined as "a judgment of the trustworthiness or goodness of a piece of research."[38] Validation encompasses various techniques, but "structural corroboration "is particularly helpful for this research. Structural corroboration is "when the researcher relates multiple types of data to support or contradict the interpretation."[39]

Another important approach which differs from validation but is still relevant for this research is the Wolcott's approach. This approach, seek first and foremost at gaining an understanding of the subject. For Creswell Wolcott's goal was to identify "critical elements" and write "plausible interpretation from them."[40] He asserts that "Wolcott ultimately tried to understand rather than convince, and he voiced the view that validation distracted from his work of understanding what was really going on."[41] For this research, a similar approach will also be employed. These previously cited processes would help mitigate any bias in this research.

The information provided by authors, although reflecting their own opinions, is also valuable for this study. It will help to explore the views of more than one author to get a broader perspective, but also to avoid as much as possible any subjectivity at the issues. According to Torill Moen "creating a narrative is primarily a process that organizes human experiences into meaningful episodes."[42] Therefore, for this research, a number of themes derived from the data, and with causal link will be analyzed. This approach will help to obtain an understanding of the various steps which led to the emergence of Alshabab in Somalia.

## Conclusion

The qualitative methodology and the narrative research method are particularly suited for this research which aims to understand the emergence of Alshabab in Somalia. Examining the historical context is necessary to grasp the emergence of this radical Islamist movement in Somalia. Creswell's extensive description of the various approaches in qualitative methodology and narrative method is useful to process the numerous Data collected. However to interpret these data objectively is a challenge, which can be mitigated by presenting only a "discourse"[43] open to reinterpretation.

[1]Catherine Marshall and Gretchen B. Rossman, *Designing Qualitative Research,* 3rd ed. (London: Sage Publications, 1999), 34.

[2]John W. Creswell, *Qualitative Inquiry and Research Design: Choosing Among Five Approaches,* 2nd ed. (London: Sage Publication, 2007), 54.

[3]Ibid., 55.

[4]Ibid.

[5]Ibid.

[6]Ibid., 56.

[7]Ibid.

[8]Ibid.

[9]Ibid., 46.

[10]Ibid.

[11]Ibid., 57.

[12]Ibid., 55.

[13]Torill Moen, "Reflections on the Narrative Research Approach," *International Journal of Qualitative Methods*, December 5, 2006, http://www.ualberta.ca/~iiqm/ backissues/5_4/pdf/moen.pdf (accessed September 10, 2011), 4.

[14]Ibid.

[15]David H. Shinn, "Al-Qaeda, Al-Shabaab and Somalia," *Mashriq Quarterly Magazine*, February 2011, http://mashriqq.com/?p=1790 (accessed June 25, 2011).

[16]Marchal, 6.

[17]Ibid, 5.

[18]Lewis, *Saints and Somalis*, 25.

[19]Ibid.

[20]Kamali, *Shari`ah Law*, 99.

[21]Ibid.

[22]Marchal, 6.

[23]Bruton, 16.

[24]Creswell, 53.

[25]Ibid., 54.

[26]Ibid.

[27]Kenneth J. Menkhaus, "Somalia and Somaliland: Terrorism, Political Islam, and State Collapse," in *Battling Terrorism in the Horn of Africa,* ed. Robert I. Rotberg (Washington, DC: Brookings Institution Press, 2005), 25.

[28]Elmi, XV.

[29]Ibid.

[30]Ibid., XVI

[31]Marchal, 4.

[32]Jean Jacques Rousseau, *The Social Contract* (United States: Pacific Publishing Studio, 2010).

[33]Thomas Hobbes, *Leviathan* (Mineola, New York: Dover Publications, Inc., 2006), 93.

[34]Ibid., 96.

[35]Ibid., 57.

[36]Ibid.

[37]Ibid., 211.

[38]Ibid., 205.

[39]Ibid., 204.

[40]Ibid., 205.

[41]Ibid.

[42]Moen, 6.

[43]Ibid., 231.

# CHAPTER 4

## ANALYSIS

In this chapter, the analysis of the data collected will be conducted in order to answer the first and second research questions. The aim of this thesis is to understand the emergence of Alshabab in Somalia. As described in the preceding chapter, this research was conducted in the framework of the qualitative methodology, and the narrative method. As Creswell pointed out "the research question should drive the data collection and analysis rather than the reverse being the case."[1] The main challenge of this research is the exclusive use of secondary documents and the difficulty inherent in the topic. To mitigate any bias, the opinion of various authors is recalled in this research. This will broaden the perspectives and present an interpretation of the data collected that is only a discourse open to reinterpretation. In order to understand the nature of Somalia Islamists and the emergence of Alshabab, a number of related themes will be examined in this chapter. This is what Creswell described as an analysis using "multiple levels of abstraction."[2]

It is important to examine the context in which the Islamic militancy had emerged in Somalia and the subsequent evolution of the political situation in Somalia. It appears that, broadly speaking, the Islamic militancy was a local solution to reestablish security and the rule of law. However a number of factors, both external and internal had contributed to the evolution of the political situation and the appearance of radical elements which endorsed terrorist tactics and intended to impose their own solution for Somalia.

## The Context: Anarchy and Clan competition

In this first section the focus is on the context of Somalia after the collapse of the State. The theme of the clan is central to Somali predicament. It is an issue that could not be eluded in Somalia even for the Islamic movements. Alittihad, the first Islamic armed movement with a political agenda in Somalia, was confronted with two main difficulties; liberating Somali inhabited regions in Ethiopia and striving to establish an Islamic state. It was a twofold strategy which turned to be fatal for the movement. As mentioned by Shaul Shay, Ethiopia, while directly sending its troops in Somalia to destroy Alittihad strong hold in 1996 and 1997, also supported clan based factions to defeat the Islamic movement.[3] Alittihad proved unable to counter this strategy, due to a lack of consistency from its leaders who could not avoid the trap of clanship. It was less the Ethiopian forces than the clan factor who drained the Islamic movement to its knees. According to Menkhaus, Alittihad found itself in a difficult position; claiming a trans-clannishness policy and unity while at the same time using clan based policy and appointing leaders hailing from the predominant clan in the areas under their control.[4]

In Somalia, alongside the demise of the state, laws and public regulation became shattered. The clans became the only normative structure left, as a means for survival but also as the holder of minimal social ties and moral conduct.[5] The Somali society is organized in clans with numerous sub fractions which are the extension of the family ties and blood relations.[6]

The environment of the coastal plain of the Horn of Africa and the subsequent nomadic style of living favored, as described by I.M.Lewis, a segmentary lineage organization.[7] In this organization, patrilineage descent and agnate relations define the individual, his place in the society, and his relation with others.[8] Clan structure is also the source for traditional laws "heer"[9] which encompass various aspects of daily life and sanction misconduct and crime. The highest penalty is the "maag"[10] or "diyaa"; the blood money for murder or causing death by accident. The clan also provides judicial structure for conflict resolution and a decision making process through meeting called "shir." In those meetings every adult male has the right to participate and express his opinion, making Somalis, according to Lewis, a "democratic and egalitarian society."[11]

Despite the fact that Somalis share relatively the same traditions, compliance to the custom of law and to moral conduct are more effective inside the clan. There have always been major difficulties to enforce the custom of law across clan spectrum mainly due to competition for grazing and water resources and to the lack of central authority.[12] The colonial era and the advent of Somali state was the only period in which Somalis have been under a central power.

The collapse of the State exacerbated the traditional competition between clans. Furthermore, the availability of modern weapons coupled with the emergence of power hungry warlords made the situation worst.[13] The traditional system has failed, at least in the South, to quell the infighting between the armed factions competing for power and even between the same clansmen. An example of this failure is the case of the Hawiye clan from which hailed the main warlords who fought for the control of Mogadishu.[14]

The clan factor was the major hurdle for any Islamic militancy and the main hindrance for Alittihad to expand in Somalia.[15] According to Menkhaus, in the regions controlled by the Islamic militancy, the challenge came from the local clans who were suspicious of the armed members of the movement who hailed from rival's clan.[16] This sentiment was fueled and manipulated by faction leaders who saw the Islamic group as an obstacle to gain power. Clan based factions such as the Somali Salvation Democratic Front (SSDF) defeated Alittihad in the northeastern port town of Bosaso.[17] According to Shay, from the year 1996 onward, the movement's leadership decided to change strategy and "withdraw from direct military activity."[18] A similar account is given in a fifty part memoir written in Somali, under the pseudonym of Abu Ibrahim. The author claimed to be a former militant of Alittihad, and his memoir was published by Somali websites supportive to Alshabab.[19] Although the objectivity and partiality of his account could be questioned, the fact that this document is published by Islamist websites gives it some credit.[20]

In late 1990s Alittihad disbanded its troops, and ordered its fighters to disarm and return to the region of their clan origin. However, as claimed by Abu Ibrahim, all members did not accept this outcome.[21] As stated also by David Shinn, a few senior members and many young fighters decided to strive to rebuild a movement dedicated to the jihad.[22] Compelled to return to their region of origin, these individuals started to organize militias. Some of these individuals are Aden Ashi Ayro, who was one of the founders of Alshabab and Daher Aweys the former head of the military wing of Alittihad. Ayro was killed in May 2008 by an US air strike in Somalia.[23] He was suspected of having links with al-Qaida and being involved in the terrorist attack on US embassies in Kenya and Tanzania in 1998.[24]

<u>A Narrative of the Genesis of Alshabab: The UIC, the Ethiopian Invasion,</u>
<u>and the Djibouti Peace Process</u>

In this second section the specific historical facts related to the genesis of

Alshabab will be examined. According to Shinn, it is in 2003 that the idea of a jihadi

organization started to take shape among individuals who decided to play a more

proactive role in Somalia. A large meeting took place in a town in Somaliland called Las

Anod.[25] It was a reunion between members of Alittihad and sympathizers but dissension

was soon aroused about the pursuit of political goals and military action.

The senior members of Alittihad, reiterated their commitment for a peaceful

agenda, as decided in late 1990s after the military defeat of the organization.[26] This

decision created dissention and many young individual held another meeting in the same

town where they discussed the way to continue the jihad in Somalia. They devised a

strategy of gaining power and competing with the warlords. According to Roland

Marshal, a senior research fellow at the French National Centre for Scientific Research

(Centre Nationale de la Recherche Scientifique or CNRS), Alshabab is the product of the

unification of four Somali groups:

> Al-Shabaab is a movement that merged four Somali groups and has been
> supported from its early days by foreign Islamists, including those linked to al-
> Qaidah. The four trends were a radical faction of Salafi Islamist group al-I'tisaam
> ( a heir of al-Itihaad), some Islamist who wanted the Islamic Courts to be military
> more efficient, Takfir wa Hijra and a cluster of Somali militants who had had an
> international experience of Jihad either in Afghanistan or elsewhere in the Arab
> world ( maybe also in Chechnya).[27]

In an interview given to Aljazeera in 2009, Mukhtar Robow, the former speaker of

Alshabab and a senior member of the organization, recalled the creation of the

movement.[28] He said that the group was formed by an association of individuals sharing

the same goal which is to establish sharia law in Somalia. He added that a number of individuals like him who returned to Somalia from Afghanistan after the US led invasion and the subsequent defeat of the Taliban has met with others in Somalia. They shared the same views on the Somali situation and the need for an armed struggle as the way to establish an Islamic state.[29]

## The Rise of the Union of Islamic Court (UIC)

As mentioned by Shay, in July 2005 Aden Hashi Ayro was appointed commander of the military wing of the UIC.[30] It was the beginning of the emergence of Alshabab, composed of young militia men who shared the same proactive approach of implementing sharia.[31] For them the uprising of the population against the warlords was a long awaited opportunity. The powerful message of unity presented to the population by the Islamic militancy was largely welcomed. This unity soon became materialized when all road blocks were lifted, and the port and the airport were reopened after fifteen years of civil wars.[32] But above all it was the security established so rapidly which further promoted support of the population. As pointed out by Shay, the disarmament of clan based militias was the key method for restoring security.[33] Furthermore any crime was faced with harsh penalties according to sharia laws.

This strict application of the Islamic code of conduct and Islamic law was sometimes the source of dissatisfaction from the population as illustrated by the episode on the ban on watching the world cup match.[34] The leadership of the UIC tried to reassure the people and minimize these acts.[35] Sheikh Sharif Sheikh Ahmad, the executive leader gave several interviews in which he tried to cast a more moderate image of the UIC.[36]

43

Another factor that contributed to the security but raised disagreement from the population was the ban on "Kat" a widely used plant in the Horn of Africa as a stimulant.[37] The Kat is legal in Ethiopia, Djibouti, Yemen and Kenya. This plant is part of the socio-economical life of the people of the region, and the trade of Kat is a source of job creation, particularly at the retail-level. However, Kat is blamed for having a negative impact on family income and on the environment, as well as diverting land that could be used for crops and fruits production.[38] Kat induces euphoria, and in Somalia it was the source of most of the acts of banditry.

The numerous checkpoints in Mogadishu were a source of revenue for the militia men who heavily taxed the vehicles to buy the narcotic. In addition to that the "moryan" (bandits) attacked the commoners to fulfill their need and afford buying the narcotic. The "Kat" trade was a booming business in Somalia and a heavily controlled one by armed factions. The ban on "Kat" while reinforcing the discipline among militia men eliminated unnecessary needs and avoided a waste of resources. Despite these above mentioned unpopular rulings, according to Afyare, the civilians welcomed the UIC: "The UIC also started cleaning the streets with the help of local people and school children. After the UIC's victory, warlordism, piracy and political assassinations ended. Overall, women, children, the elderly, unarmed clans, and civilians appreciated and welcomed this change."[39]

<u>The Ethiopian military intervention and the defeat of the UIC</u>

The Ethiopian military action in Somalia and the subsequent defeat of the UIC is an important theme in understanding the gradual emergence of Alshabab as an autonomous movement. According to Shay, after their victory over the warlords in

Mogadishu, the challenge for the UIC was "to extend and broaden the organization without being weakened by inter-clan politics."[40] They set up ad hoc political institutions in order to build the framework of a functioning government. They established the Islamic Supreme Consultation Council of Islamic Courts or Supreme Islamic Courts Council (SICC).[41] This council, known as "Shura" was composed of 91 members who acted as a parliament and it had no executive powers.[42] The decisions were implemented by an executive committee of 15 members chaired by Sheikh Sharif.[43] According to Shay the replacement of Sheikh Sharif as leader of the UIC by Dahir Aweys, in June 2006, showed that the more radical element took power over the UIC.[44] However, Sheikh Sharif remained a key leader in the organization.

If there were dissensions they were less visible than the growing misunderstandings between the UIC and the TFG headed by Abdullahi Youssouf. Discussions were organized in Khartoum between the TFG and UIC however; those efforts of mediation were hindered by the growing mistrust between the two sides.[45] One of the key issues was the deployment of a peacekeeping force.[46] During the last months of 2006, both sides blamed the other for the failure of the negotiations; the TFG accused the Islamists of conducting military actions and advancing while the UIC denounced the increasing number of Ethiopian troops penetrating the country.[47].

In September 2006 after the UIC forces took the port town of Kismayo, controlled by militia men loyal to Barre Hiirale the defense minister of the TFG, all talks were halted.[48] The UIC suspecting the TFG of the intention to request Ethiopian military intervention moved its forces closer to Baidoa to begin the siege of the transitional institutions. Fearing the imminent fall of the TFG, and as mentioned by Elmi, perceiving

45

the Islamists as a threat to its national security, Ethiopian forces invaded Somalia and defeated the UIC in December 2006.[49]

The leadership of the UIC fled the country, and most of them went to Eritrea. The latter gained its independence in 1991 after a three decades long conflict with Ethiopia. As pointed out by Dan Connell in *Battling Terrorism in the Horn of Africa*, "during its first decade as a recognized state, Eritrea careened from one armed conflict with its neighbors to another, while sliding ever deeper into political repression and economic malaise."[50] An unresolved border issue with Ethiopia led to a major military confrontation in 1999.[51] As mentioned by Bruton "a cease-fire has held since 2000, but both sides have continued their dispute through proxy warfare."[52] For Eritrea, welcoming the UIC leadership was a means for pressuring Ethiopia. The young fighters, Alshabab regrouped in the South and they vowed to fight against the invaders. Many Somalis inside the country and abroad were alarmed by the invasion, and as mentioned by Bruton, Alshabab received strong support for waging this insurgency.[53]

The TFG, despite defeating the UIC and seizing Mogadishu could not capitalize on the new situation. The political failure of the TFG was due to the fact that the TFG from its formation in Mbagathi,[54] Kenya, did not reflect the true will of the Somali people despite the two years spent on its creation. It was generated by a top-down process which lacked the legitimacy that more inclusive discussions conducted in Somalia could have produced. The parliament who elected Abdullahi Youssouf[55] (former head of the SSDF faction) in Nairobi, Kenya, was composed of individuals hand-picked in political negotiations. Many were head of armed clan-based factions as pointed out by Elmi:

At the outset, there were serious problems with the process that produced Somalia's Transitional Federal Government. Ethiopia dominated the peace process. In particular, it rewarded the warlords that supported its policies by appointing them as members of the parliament and cabinet, and it punished those who were not on its side: civil society, nationalist intellectuals, and Islamists. Since representation problems have always been the most difficult challenge, Ethiopia and Kenya, with the help of IGAD, arbitrarily selected most of the 275 members of the parliament. They also alienated factions and countries that were important for any successful peace agreement in Somalia.[56]

The TFG became entangled in the insurgency war and it was seen as a collaborator of the occupiers. Ethiopian forces withdrawn from Somalia in January 2009 after a period of occupation considered as one of the bloodiest in Somalia history.[57] Before its involvement Ethiopia did not expect a long war as Meles Zenawi, Ethiopia premier minister stated: "We are planning to stay there for a month, hopefully it would be completed in days, if not a few weeks at most, but once we have done that we are out of it."[58]

According to Bruton the Ethiopian withdrawal was caused by the failure of the TFG to gain support from the population, and for Ethiopia, the unsustainable "costs of confronting the growing Islamist insurgency in Mogadishu."[59] Misreading the nature and the objective of Somali Islamism and the perception of a threat from the UIC led to these unfortunate events. Ethiopia did not take into consideration the popular nature of the uprising against the warlords in Mogadishu that brought the UIC to power.

The object of the Ethiopian worry is the Somali inhabited regions, which have been shaped for decades by a secessionist movement. These regions were conquered for the most part by Emperor Menelik[60] of Ethiopia in the late nineteenth century and the other part (Haud region) was given to Ethiopia by Britain after World War II. Ethiopia feared that a hostile government in Somalia may reinforce this secessionist movement

47

and provide them substantial support. The truth is no referendum or poll was ever organized to let the Somali people in the Ethiopia controlled region expressed their views on the question.

The principle of the intangibility of the frontier was inherited from the colonial past and proclaimed in 1964, has been proven unrealistic, and was breached in recent years by the independence of Eritrea, in 1992. The most recent breach to this principle was the case of the South Sudan where the January 2011 referendum showed unanimity for independence. This fear of a hostile Somali government dominated by Islamists was publicly expressed by Ethiopian authorities, as noted by Elmi:

> Ethiopia has released a document it calls 'Ethiopia's Policy Toward Somalia,' in which it articulates its interests and goals as they relate to Somalia. Ethiopia acknowledges its hostile attitude toward Somalia during the Siyad Barre era, arguing that Somalia was a source for many of Ethiopia's problems. Moreover, Ethiopia justifies its actions by claiming that pan-Somali-nationalism and Islamist projects are threats to its national security interest.[61]

It is a display of what is call in the field of international relations, "Hobbesian Realism."[62] The Ethiopia intervention against the UIC also precluded a golden opportunity to stabilize Somalia. It was the first time in 16 years that clan division was transcended and a new political class of Somalis different from the infamous warlords emerged. Perhaps the most significant consequence of the Ethiopian intervention is the empowerment of the Alshabab which emerged as an autonomous organization.[63]

### The Djibouti Peace Process and the New TFG

After the invasion, Somalis inside and outside the country begin to mobilize themselves and this mobilization generated the creation of the Alliance for the Re-liberation of Somalia (ARS). An opposition movement composed of disaffected MPs,

48

senior leadership of the defeated UIC, and the Somalis diaspora.[64]Meanwhile the

insurgency increased its activities despite the deployment in May 2007 of African Union

forces in an attempt by the international community to reinforce the legality and

legitimacy of the TFG. Parallel to that a renewed attempt to end the political deadlock

started. Djibouti initiated mediation in 2008 with the full benediction of the UN who

delegated a special representative, Ambassador Ould Abdallah, UN Representative of the

Secretary General (SRSG).[65] According to Meredith Preston McGhie, a senior UN

official who participated in the process, the aim was to allow the opposing parties to meet

on neutral ground suited for serene dialogue where mutual trust could be built and

discussion on contentious points could be envisaged. A formal adherence to an agenda

supervised by third parties assured that both parties were committed to advances in the

talks. As McGhie recounted the fundamental approach of the Djibouti negotiations were

based on flexibility and constructiveness:

> While there was no formalized strategy for the mediation Ambassador Ould
> Abdallah had a vision of where he wanted to direct the talks. From a tactical
> perspective four key principles threaded through the process and dictated how it
> played out: 1) the constructive use of deadlines to push the process along
> (although control over the deadlines, crucially, was lost in January 2009). 2)
> building a mechanism that would allow Somali leadership and ownership.3)
> managing regional and international actors.4) ensuring flexibility to respond and
> adapt to the changing situation.[66]

The Djibouti peace process generated renewed transitional institutions with the

integration in the parliament of 275 new members from the opposition and the election of

a new president. The new TFG has a mandate of two years starting in 2009. Its goals and

its missions were to broaden reconciliation talks even with the different autonomous

regions. At the end of the two year period the TFG would have created a constitution and

elections would have been prepared to ensure a peaceful transfer of power and a change of leadership. Despite the fact that it took one year to be completed, the Djibouti peace process is criticized as having moved too fast.[67]

External events put pressure on the process, such as the increasing insurgency action and the resignation of President Abdullah Hassan who was opposed to the peace process. The main failure of the Djibouti peace process is to not have engaged enough with the armed opposition elements such as Alshabab, who composed the main forces in the insurgency. The problem is that not enough considerations were given to the refusals of the insurgency to any foreign presence. The consequences were crippling for the new TFG which spent the next two years entangled in a conflict which impeded it from imposing itself and establishing collective services and security.

### Restorying the data collected: Grasping the nature of Alshabab, its major mistakes, and evaluating the military approach of its opponents

In this third section, the analysis of the various themes narrated previously, will be conducted in order to shed light on the characteristic of the Alshabab phenomenon. During the last two years Alshabab has expanded despite the efforts of the new TFG to counter the Islamic militancy. As noted by Bruton, Alshabab succeeded in controlling almost the entire South of Somalia.[68] The expansion and the control by Alshabab of these wide regions with many localities and a key port could not have been possible if the group had not gained support from the population.

Although Alshabab rule is an authoritarian one, they have succeeded in establishing security and the rule of law (sharia) in the area under their control. Somali society is an egalitarian society which its customs dwell from a nomadic style of living which favor freedom and independence. In such an environment a single organization could not control such a wide region without providing some response to local needs.

Force is not the only explanation to Alshabab successes. Their doctrine and their methods have something inherent that responded in some ways to the grievances of the population. According to Christopher Anzalone the control of territories presents to insurgent movement "a unique set of challenges" concerning the way to administer these territories and the relationship with the population.[69] Anzalone claims that Alshabab is also faced with the same challenges and it is aware of the need for public support:

> On the one hand it (*Alshabab*) has not established an inclusive system of governance and it enforces a harsh interpretation of Islamic law, including the carrying out of public executions, floggings, and amputations as punishments for a range of crimes from murder to rape, spying and theft. On the other hand, Harakat al-Shabaab has not been completely oblivious to the need for it to establish some type of governance and outreach, or public relations, with the local population in territories it governs. Indeed, it has been active in publicizing its ongoing distribution of aid to the drought-stricken regions of southern and central Somalia.[70]

In order to obtain support from the population and as mentioned by Christopher Anzalone "Harakat al-Shabaab has also been undertaking small and medium-sized public works projects since at least 2009."[71] Alshabab's main strength is its ability to maintain order. By enforcing the Sharia and its harsh sanctions, Alshabab casts a message which is powerful enough to deter any criminal act.[72] Emulating the same method used by the UIC, Alshabab removed road blocks and favored the circulation of people and goods. But along the way, individual liberties were reduced such as the interdiction of music or playing soccer and the imposition of the "hijab" (the veil) for women.

It seems that this is the price that the Islamic movement wants people to pay for preserving the most important rights, the right for one to live, to work and to enjoy their properties which were in jeopardy for more than two decades. Sharia laws are very harsh on crime and the severity of its penalties and the public character of the punishments are meant to be dissuasive. And despite its severity, Alshabab enforced Sharia law as a remedy to lawlessness and anarchy, which were perpetuated by warlords.

One of the long term consequences of the venality of these warlords is that Somalia was used as a toxic dump.[73] Some toxic-waste was simply dumped on the coastline while other times it was buried on shore. This lawlessness has also made the coast of Somali an area suitable for illegal fishing, inducing the piracy which started first as a reaction for self-defense against this illegal fishing before become a booming business as mentioned by Elmi:

> Piracy off the coast of Somalia has been the direct result of the increased illegal fishing and toxic-waste dumping in Somali waters. Somali pirates have spoken of the abuses committed against local Somali fishermen by foreign vessels fishing illegally in the area. According to the UN Food and Agriculture Organization, more than 700 foreign vessels have been fishing illegally in Somali waters since 2005.[74]

One of the most important factors that explain the support that Alshabab received is that the restoration of security in the regions under their control allowed the reemergence of commerce and trade. The implementation of sharia law has reduced the risk of robbery as well as the need for the business community to keep armed men. In a context of collapsed states the implementation of sharia law and the subsequent security obtained explains why a significant segment of Somali population supported the Islamist movement. According to radio Shabelle, a neutral media in Mogadishu, some business men acknowledged the safe environment existing in the areas under Alshabab control and particularly in Bakara market.[75] This market is the main trade center of Mogadishu and home for several telecom companies.

The application of "Hudud"; sharia law penalties, is seen as barbaric in the west and even among Somalis who never applied it despite being Muslims for centuries. The traditional laws; "Heer" are more flexible and do not include any amputation whatsoever or public flagellation. The Koran exhorts men to apply the "Hudud" (sanctions) which are God's commandments, emphasizing also on the dissuasive aspect: "As to the thief, male or female, cut off his or her hands, a retribution for their deed and exemplary punishment from Allah and Allah is exalted in power, full of wisdom"(5:38). The "Qisas" (talion) or death penalty for a murderer is also explicated in the following verse: "In Qisas there is (saving of) life for you: O you men of understanding." (2:179)

The adoption of Islamic principles as a rule of law is a trend in Somalia which increasingly becomes generalized from the late 1990s due to its result on the ground. The earlier sharia courts established in each clan controlled area had tremendous difficulty in fully applying the sharia universally and not inside the clan only. And it seems that Alshabab like the UIC has transcended clan divisions and succeeded in implementing the Islamic law in the regions under their control. However, Alshabab despite becoming the icon of the resistance against Ethiopian invasion and restoring security fell into the trap of the authoritarism and extremism. By refusing to take part in the Djibouti peace process they also indicated an uncompromising view of politics. This stand could be interpreted as a political mistake showing their inability to conceive of power sharing and plurality. But it is also a strong indication of their ideology and political doctrine.

Alshabab rejected any democratic system of governance based on the western model of the separation of power as executive, legislative and judicial and the organization of elections. Moreover, they rejected any constitution or man-made laws as a basis for societal regulation and political mechanisms. Their refusal on the Djibouti negotiations showed also their suspicion of the Somali politicians. Half of the MPs are the same ones who cautioned against the Ethiopian invasion, and a significant number of the defeated warlords are also members of the parliament. This raises the question of impunity in regards to the responsibility of these warlords in the bloodshed which took place in the country. Former warlords who are now MPs are Mohamed Qanyare Afreh, Mousse Sudi Yalhow, Osman Ato, and Barre Hirale. No judicial mechanisms have been discussed to put these warlords on trial; it has never been on the agenda of Djibouti peace process and neither or any previous conference agenda. Their status as MPs is an indication that the representatives in the parliament have not been elected, but they have been appointed in political bargaining and power brokering involving the neighboring countries. Another point which may explain the refusal of Alshabab to participate in the political game is the disillusionment with the first TFG of president Abdusalam Salat Hassan elected in Arta, Djibouti in 2000. The sharia courts existing at that time released their Islamic militia in order to form a new security force for the new government. But the TFG met with difficulty and become entangled in the clan based Somali political life which impeded it from expanding its control. Another important factor which explains the hardline stand taken by Alshabab is their alignment with al-Qaida and the global jihad. This alliance has made Alshabab to adhere to global jihad and incorporate the Somali case in the wider context of the struggle against western interests and presence in Muslim countries while reforming the Muslim societies. The rejection by Alshabab of a parliamentary system and the suspicions on the politicians could have been resolved in negotiation and reconciliation. However their alliance with al-Qaida has made Alshabab anathema not only among Somalis but also in the local region and beyond.

## The Strategic mistakes of *Alshabab*

Alshabab has shown that it is capable of restoring security but it has also shown its rejection of political pluralism. The organization has made several mistakes detrimental to its control and its expansion in Somalia, and for the promotion of its doctrine. Rousseau writes: "the strongest is never strong enough to be always the master, unless he transforms strength into right, and obedience into duty."[76] Alshabab proved that it could defeat any clan- based armed group because it has a message of unity and it applies an already existing law, the sharia. The problem is they are at the same time ruler, magistrate and legislator and the population is left with no mechanism to control its ruler. Their conception of sovereignty is that only God is sovereign and the will of the people has to abide of God's will manifested by his commandment; the sharia law. It is a simplistic view on politics that could easily lead to totalitarianism. This view does not take in consideration that the temporal character of any government even based on religious laws necessitate the accountability of those who are charged to implement the law. It is the only guarantee for justice no matter how righteous the judge is. And this accountability is due to the people for whose benefit the laws are. It is also the basis for legitimacy. A close examination of the main source of Islamic principles; the Koran, shows that absolutism is discouraged and the will of the people that Alshabab disregards is given predominance in Islam as the following verse shows: "Let there be no compulsion in religion, truth stand out clear from error" (2:256). Therefore, according to this verse, freedom of choice is given to individual in accepting religion it may be

55

deduced that is the same for political matters as seem to be confirmed by the Islamic principle of "Shura"; consultation in temporal matters.

Another major mistake made by Alshabab was to radically oppose religious – based customs such as veneration of saints and celebration of the birth of prophet Mohamed. Their radical interpretation of Islam became epitomized when Alshabab members destroyed Sufi saint's graves. These repeated acts have generated large opposition and demonstrations against Alshabab. It resulted in the creation of Ahlu Suna Wal Jama'a (ASWJ). It is an armed movement formed by several clans claiming Sufi heritage and dedicated to confront militarily Alshabab radicalism. Somalis adhere to the Shafi'i rites of the Sharia[77] which is one of the four schools of thought or 'madhab' in the Sunni branch of Islam. The three other are Hanafi, Maliki, and Hanbali. Somalis also adhere to the Sufi current in Islam, which is a revivalist movement that arose and developed between the 9th and 13th centuries.[78] Sufism has been introduced by the 'Tariqa' (path) which were dedicated to spread the teaching of Islam.[79] These 'Tariqa' were organized in congregations and they are now an integral part of Somali culture. Sufi is described as an esoteric movement and its practices are marked by mysticism and the remembrance of God through "Dikhr," the goal being to reach a higher level of spirituality; the "Mari'fa" (absorption in god or gnosis).[80] Regular pilgrimages are made to celebrate the memories of the earliest saint founders of these 'Tariqa.' For Alshabab to take on this centuries long practice was equal as to declaring war on Somalis culture and identity. It was a strategic mistake and one of the symbols of Alshabab radicalism.

One more important mistake was the adoption of terrorist tactics. Alshabab has carried out more than 26 major suicide attacks in Somalia since September 2006.[81] This number is likely to rise as the recent offensive of the TFG as caused some setbacks to the movement. The bombing of the hotel Shamo on December 3, 2009 was one of the deadliest suicide bombings in Somalia. This bombing which took place at a graduation ceremony for young medical graduates killed 25 people. Most of those killed were students; among the dead were two doctors, three journalists, and three government ministers. The president of the TFG, sheikh Sharif called this attack a "national disaster."[82] Alshabab spokesman, Sheikh Mahamoud Rage held a press conference and released a statement in which the group denied responsibility for this act and accused some members of the government for having masterminded a plot. The modus operandi was similar to the previous attacks that the group has carried out and despite their denials everything pointed in their direction. It could be also be an indication of the decentralized structure of the group and the existence of even more hard-line factions inside the group. The influence of foreign fighters has been blamed for the adoption by Alshabab of Taliban like tactics and the adherence to the global jihad ideology. The senior leadership of Alshabab has been trained in Afghanistan and their adherence to violent actions dwell from this experience. Analysts believe that there is a growing dissent inside the movement.[83] Some key issues are the role of the foreigners and the overall objectives of the movement. Robow is assumed to be second in command, and he is seen as less radical. He is himself is a veteran from Afghanistan but he has criticized on several occasions actions attributed to the groups such as the acts of destroying tombs that he qualified as premature and susceptible to generate hostilities towards the group from the general population.[84] Shinn reported also that dissensions have risen within the group concerning the policy toward Hizbul Islam and Daher Aweys.[85] The merger between the two groups in December 2010 has put an end to the speculation about disagreements within the group.

But the existence of different opinions inside the movement shows that Alshabab is less rigid than it appears. Roland Marshall pointed out that "the public expression of internal dissidence should not be overestimated compared to the other challenges faced by Alshabab: the drought that pushed many people to leave areas controlled by Alshabab and the ideological defeat within Salafi Islam."[86] The internal organization of the movement provides also the mechanism for discussions. According to Marshal, a council known as Shura does exist:

> The top leadership structure is the Shura. This institution functions by consensus since it endorses a Quranic prescription (see Sura 3, Verse 159). Its mandate is to discuss all important issues concerning the organization, ideological, political, or military. Its membership is not known for sure. Al-Shabaab websites keep quoting its decisions and views but never ever provided its number and membership. Educated guesses go often to 31 members but some observers add that after the merging with Hisbul Islam it grew up to 53. Rumors say that foreigners are included in the Shura but one may wonder in which language the discussions take place.[87]

However this Shura has a more consultative role than anything else and as Marshal writes "the Shura might not be the most relevant in terms of decision making, whatever al-Shabaab websites claim. One of its main roles is to dilute the recurrent question on clanship."[88] Marshall describes the movement as a "decentralized organization as opposed to a fragmented one."[89] The presence of foreigners has been important for Alshabab in order to obtain financial support and needed skills. The alignment with al-Qaida and the message of ben laden to support the Somalis mujahidin has been beneficial for the group in terms of financial support. But it has been counterproductive in terms of

Somali support and it raised regional awareness in the neighboring countries which perceive Alshabab as a threat.

## The logic of war

Alshabab has refused any offers of dialogue from the TFG compelling it to choose by default a military solution. In fact it was not until after the deadliest attack on the graduation ceremonies in December 2009 that all prospect of talks disappeared. The TFG allied with others groups in order to crush militarily the Islamic militancy. The main allies with the TFG in this conflict are Ahlu Sunna Wal Jama'a (ASWJ) and the Ras Kamboni. These groups claim a religious oriented purpose and their aim is to defeat Alshabab and its radical ideology. They present themselves as nationalist opposed to the foreign fighters that Alshabab has brought into Somalia. Both of these groups are opposed to the jihadist agenda advocated by Alshabab. In February these groups launched a coordinated attack alongside some forces of the TFG from the Kenya and Ethiopia border in the South of Somalia. ASWJ is openly supported by Ethiopia which provides them weapons and ammunition while the Ras Kamboni forces are supported by the Kenyan government. In a few weeks they have made substantial territorial gains by conquering several border towns controlled by Alshabab.

In April, their offensive seemed to culminate due to lack of manpower and enough supplies. It also seems that internal rivalries and clan divisions have hindered them from making further gains. Internal clashes even erupted indicating that their coalition was very fragile. But above all, the biggest hurdle for them is the lack of a common command center. There is no unity of command which could ensure unity of effort. It became clear that what is uniting them is having a common enemy more than a real political objective. Even inside each of these groups, the power sharing based on clan is a source of trouble and continuous feuding. The larger group, ASWJ, is the most susceptible to being victim of clan division due to the fragility of the alliance between the clans from which the fighters of this movement hail. They also accuse the TFG of not supporting them enough in term of supply and financial resources. The TFG has welcomed these groups and it apparently has no problem with the fact that external powers have direct relations with these groups. For the long term it is a situation which could be really problematic. It could eventually hinder the ability of the TFG to expand its control in Somalia. The new situation shows that the neighboring countries, for instance Kenya and Ethiopia have started a proxy war in Somalia to quell the expansion of Alshabab. Their goal is to preempt Alshabab influence in their territories. But such a strategy is far from being a satisfactory one. Until now, despite substantial territorial gains made by pro-governmental forces, the only tangible result achieved by the new offensive is a flow of refugees to Kenya and Ethiopia. The South has already been hit by a severe drought and when the combat started the refugee situation got worse. The strategy is also undermining the collective effort of the African Union and the international community to support the TFG and enhance its legitimacy. The increase of armed groups instead of contributing to the restoration of peace is perpetuating the civil war in Somalia. Another point is that this strategy is also favoring the propaganda of Alshabab who scathe at the presence of foreign troops and foreign intervention in Somali politics. The reinforcement of the TFG government with enough financial support to recruit and train more governmental soldiers would have been wiser.

## Conclusion

In order to understand the emergence of Alshabab, "multiple themes were combined into larger themes or perspectives," according to the Creswell's approach on narrative research method.[90] The themes narrated permit to envision the context in which Alshabab emerged. It seems that the appearance of this group in Somalia could be explained by the result of the internal evolution of the Somali socio-political environment and the impact of external factors such as the Ethiopian intervention. After the failure of the southern political leadership to resolve their differences and stop the competition for power, the Islamic movement arose in order to provide their solutions based on sharia law. While most of the Islamic movements focused on social welfare, Alittihad embarked on a fierce competition with the warlords and tried to establish an Islamist state in Somalia. This effort failed because it could not sort out the way to avoid clan issues. They also had a dual objective both in Somalia and in Ethiopia that turned out to be fatal for the movement. Despite the defeat of Alittihad, Somali society became increasingly influenced by the Islamist ideas. This could be explained by the success achieved by the earlier Islamic courts in restoring order in an anarchic environment. More sharia courts were created even in areas controlled by warlords, setting these courts in a collision course with these warlords. The confrontation took place in the end of 2005, when an alliance of warlords supported by the U.S started to hunt and arrest individuals suspected of having links with al-Qaida. The unification of all the sharia courts and the subsequent defeat of the warlords brought to power the Islamist organizations. Among them was Alshabab. It is not until the military intervention of Ethiopia and the defeat of the Union

Islamic Court, that Alshabab, having started an insurgency in Mogadishu, emerged as a true autonomous movement.

---

[1] Creswell, 211.

[2] Ibid., 46.

[3] Shay, 44.

[4] Menkhaus, 112.

[5] Lewis, *Blood and Bone*, vii.

[6] Ibid., 19.

[7] Ibid.

[8] Ibid.

[9] Ibid., 84.

[10] Ibid.

[11] Ibid., 22.

[12] Ibid., 23.

[13] Ibid., 231.

[14] Lyons and Samatar, 22.

[15] Menkhaus, 112.

[16] Ibid.

[17] Shay, 43.

[18] Ibid., 44.

[19] Abu Ibrahim, "Mad soo gaadhay Gaal iyo Wadaad Gaadh u wada tagaan" [Have you seen an Infidel and a religious man together], Amiirnuur, January 2011, http://www.amiirnuur.com/index.php?option=com_content&view=article&id=3399:ma-soo-gaadhay-gaal-iyo-wadad-gaadh-u-wada-taagan-qormadii-23-aad&catid=59:maqaallo&Itemid=86 (accessed July 1, 2011).

[20] Somalimemo has also published all part of Abu Ibrahim memoir.

[21]Abu Ibrahim, 38-40.

[22]Shinn, "Al-Qaeda, Al-Shabaab and Somalia," *Mashriq Quarterly Magazine*, February 2011, http://mashriqq.com/?p=1790 (accessed July 2011).

[23]Ibid.

[24]Associated Press, "Somalia's al-Qaeda leader killed in airstrikes," *USA Today*, May 2008, http://www.usatoday.com/news/world/2008-05-01-somalia-airstrike_N.htm?csp=34 (accessed July 2011).

[25]Shinn.

[26]Shay, 44.

[27]Marchal, 4.

[28]kismaayonews.com, Interview of Mukhtar Robow by Aljazeera, translated by Sabriye Macalin Muuse, March 2009, http://kismaayonews.com/pageView.php?articleid=295 (accessed July 2011).

[29]Ibid.

[30]Shay, 94.

[31]Ibid.

[32]Elmi, 83.

[33]Shay, 99.

[34]Ibid.

[35]BBC News, "Somalia soccer shooting arrest," July 2006, http://news.bbc.co.uk/2/hi/africa/5153800.stm (accessed July 2011).

[36]Shay, 105.

[37]*The Somaliland Times*,"Khat Fight in Somalia Question Islamist Position," no. 252, http://www.somalilandtimes.net/sl/2006/252/091.shtml (accessed July 1, 2011).

[38]Trade and environment database, "TED Case Study: Qat trade in Africa," http://www1.american.edu/projects/mandala/TED/qat.htm (accessed November 10, 2011).

[39]Elmi, 84.

[40]Shay, 95.

[41]Ibid., 96.

[42]Ibid.

[43]IRIN, "Somalia: The challenge of change," July 2006, http://www.irinnews.org/PrintReport.aspx?ReportId=59567 (accessed July 2011).

[44]Shay, 106.

[45]Ibid., 111.

[46]Ibid.

[47]Shay, 101.

[48]IRIN,"Somalia: UIC disarm militia, tightens control over Kismayo," September 2006, http://www.irinnews.org/report.aspx?reportid=61203 (accessed July 2011).

[49]Elmi, 95.

[50]Dan Connell, "Eritrea: On a Slow Fuse," in *Battling Terrorism: In the Horn of Africa,* ed. Robert I. Rotberg (Washington, DC: Brookings Institution Press, 2005), 65.

[51]BBC.news, "World: Africa, Ethiopia declares victory," (March 1, 1999), http://news.bbc.co.uk/2/hi/africa/287736.stm (accessed November 10, 2011).

[52]Bruton, 17.

[53]Ibid., 8.

[54]Elmi, 23.

[55]Ibid., 60.

[56]Ibid., 23.

[57]Bruton, 9.

[58]Shay, 121.

[59]Bruton, 9.

[60]Lyons and Samatar, 11.

[61]Elmi, 96.

[62]Jack Donnelly, "Realism," in *Theories of International Relations*, 4th ed. (New York: Palgram Macmillan, 2009), 35.

[63]Ibid., 2.

[64]Meredith Preston McGuie, "Mediating Djibouti," Conciliation Resources, 2010, http://www.c-r.org/our-work/accord/somalia/mediating-djibouti.php (accessed June 11, 2011).

[65]Ibid.

[66]Ibid.

[67]Ibid.

[68]Bruton, 3.

[69]Christopher Anzalone, "Building an Insurgent State," Hiiraan Online, March 15, 2011, http://www.hiiraan.com/op2/2011/mar/building_an_insurgent_state_in_ somalia.aspx (accessed July 3, 2011).

[70]Ibid.

[71]Ibid.

[72]Anzalone.

[73]Najad Abdullahi,"Toxic Waste behind Somali Piracy," Al Jazeera English, October 2008, http://english.aljazeera.net/news/africa/2008/10/ 2008109174223218644.html (accessed July 3, 2011).

[74]Elmi, 10.

[75]Radio Shabelle, "Shabaab iyo ganacsato isku raacay inay la dagaalamaan DKMG" [Alshabab and business community agreed to resist to TFG], Radio Shabelle, May 2011, http://shabelle.net/article.php?id=7054 (accessed July 2011).

[76]Rousseau, 4.

[77]Lewis, *Saints and Somalis*, 8.

[78]Ibid.

[79]Ibid., 9.

[80]Ibid.

[81]Bill Roggio, "Shabaab suicide attack kills 20 in Somali capital," *The Long War Journal,* February 22, 2011. http://www.longwarjournal.org/archives/2011/02/ shabaab_suicide_atta_1.php (accessed June 7, 2011).

[82]BBC News," Somalia al-Shabab Islamist deny causing deadly bomb," December 4, 2009, http://news.bbc.co.uk/2/hi/africa/8394528.stm (accessed July 2011).

[83]Shinn.

[84]Kismayow.com, "Interview of Mukhtar Robow by Aljazeera," translated by Sabriye Macalin Muuse.

[85]Shinn.

[86]Marchal, 9.

[87]Ibid., 19.

[88]Ibid.

[89]Ibid., 5.

[90]Creswell, 54.

# CHAPTER 5

## CONCLUSIONS AND RECOMMENDATIONS

During the course of this research, the situation in south and central Somalia has dramatically evolved. Alshabab denial of access for the main humanitarian organizations caused a disastrous humanitarian crisis. AMISOM forces and the TFG troops pushed the radical groups out on the outskirts of the capital. Moreover the United States government resumed a campaign of drone attacks on Alshabab. The newest episode of the military escalation is that Kenya launched a military intervention inside Somalia in late October. Although not defeated yet, Alshabab has suffered some setbacks. But the organization changed its tactics and instead of holding ground, it started employing hit and run actions, and intensified its suicide attacks.

On the political level, the TFG mandate was extended for one year. The government of Prime Minister Mohamed Abdullahi[1] was toppled as the result of an agreement achieved in Kampala by the TFG president and the parliament speaker. This accord was backed by the Uganda president, Yoweri Museveni and the UN Secretary General Special Representative for Somalia, Augustine P. Mahiga. The aim was to solve the political deadlock between these two Somalis politicians who diverged on the issue of the future of the TFG whose mandate was ending in August 2011. A new Prime Minister, Abdulwali Gaas, was appointed for one year with the main task of preparing a new constitution. The TFG has also started to broaden its political sphere of influence by reaching out to other movements and political entities, particularly those in the autonomous region of Puntland. For the first time in 20 years, a consultative conference between Somali political groups was held in Mogadishu in September 2011. It seems that the TFG has made significant gains politically as well as militarily. However, the root causes of the Somali predicament are not yet solved. The recent military success is to be attributed primarily to the credit of AMISOM who adopted a more aggressive stance rather than to a real buildup of TFG forces. The issue of Alshabab's armed opposition is still unresolved, militarily or politically. As narrated in the previous chapters, this examination conducted on the currently available data permit one to assert that at least two categories of factors, internal and external, caused the emergence of Alshabab.

### Internal Factors: The collapse of the State and the expansion of islamist ideas

The collapse of the Somali state resulted in the destruction of all public structures as well as all judicial and political institutions. The people in the north of Somalia achieved a successful reconciliation process that led to the creation of two autonomous regions, Puntland and Somaliland. The leadership of the south failed to facilitate a similar process, and in Mogadishu, general Aided and Ali Mahdi fought for years despite both of them hailing from the same Hawiye clan. Amidst the ensuing anarchy and chaos prevailing in the south, Islamist movements begin to organize themselves. Alittihad distinguished itself from other Islamist movements by its political agenda and its intention of competing with the armed factions. However a dual objective; waging jihad both in Ethiopia and Somalia, and the lack of a clear strategy undermined its expansion. The group was finally defeated militarily by Ethiopian forces and their Somali allies. Meanwhile, the intervention of the international community during Operation Restore Hope and the following UNOSOM missions helped to provide urgent humanitarian aid but failed to stabilize the country. Despite the defeat of Alitthad, the Islamist ideas

68

continued to spread as well as Islamic charities and relief organizations. These organizations made significant contributions in reducing human suffering and promoting education.[2] Soon the need for justice and stability led to the implementation of sharia law even in warlord controlled areas. The initial success of the Islamic courts contributed to the spread of other Islamic courts in Mogadishu as well as in other parts of south and central Somalia.

External Factors: Al-Qaida ideology and
Ethiopian military intervention

After September 2001, the US started its global war on terror (GWOT). In Somalia, the US government sponsored a group of Mogadishu based warlords to search and arrest any individual linked with al-Qaida. These warlords created the Alliance for Restoration of Peace and Counter Terrorism (ARPCT). The actions of this alliance were seen as despicable by the population. In a few months all the Islamic courts united and with the help of the population, defeated all the Mogadishu warlords and faction leaders. The UIC unified Mogadishu, after 16 years of civil war. However, a cluster of young individuals with a radical agenda also played a significant role in these events. This radical group, known as Alshabab, pushed toward a confrontation with the weak TFG of Abdullahi Youssouf based in Badoia. The fear of Somalia falling into the hands of these Islamists prompted Ethiopia to act. In December 2006, Ethiopian forces invaded Somalia, defeated the UIC militias, and took control of Mogadishu. The main consequence of this intervention was the demise of the UIC and the emergence of Alshabab as an autonomous organization.

## Political deadlock

Alshabab's uncompromising stance on politics and its terrorist methods made any dialogue with them quite impossible. The TFG was compelled to confront the Islamist movement militarily. For almost two years, AMISOM and the governmental security forces were on the defensive. The TFG was restricted to a small perimeter in Mogadishu and under constant attack. Alshabab could have imposed a number of conditions favorable to it on the TFG if the group had been willing to negotiate a peace settlement.

Alshabab controlled a wide area and authors such as Roland Marshal acknowledged that their internal bureaucratic structure was unlike other Somali movements.[3] Whether by default or resulting from a deliberate program Alshabab had set up an administrative structure in the areas under their control. The movement has also a government like structure, the "Maktab," which are equivalent of ministries and are responsible for policies in various fields such as defense, education, charities, and political affairs.[4] Alshabab has also established an administrative provincial delimitation, the "Wilayat," and has appointed regional governors.

Despite these structures which suggest that the movement has undeniable political ambitions, the Alshabab political agenda for Somalia is yet to be seen. The organization has not formulated an official political program with the goal of rebuilding the Somalia State, even in an Islamic form. Alshabab discourse does not go beyond the paradigm of jihad and the implementation of the sharia. This lack of political program coupled with their silence concerning any roadmap for building an Islamic State in Somalia, is the principal weakness of Alshabab. It could also be an indication of an ideological inflexibility. Alshabab does not consider its opponents as political adversaries but as "apostates." The radicalization of the political discourse in Somalia has further impeded any perspective of agreement. Transposing from the religious dimension into the political field is a challenge that Alshabab will face sooner or later. Unless the movement undertakes this evolution, its military and political survival will be uncertain as its opposition becomes more organized.

## Recommendations

The clan competition resulting from the collapse of the Somali state and foreign intervention have been determinant for Alshabab to gain support. In order to promote its radical ideology, Alshabab needs these two factors. As long as its opponent will be divided along clan lines and as long as foreign forces will be present in Somalia, Alshabab will be able to justify its jihad, based on its interpretation of the Quran. Alshabab is able to gain support with a simple unifying message with a strong religious appeal in a context of a clan competition and a collapsed state; unity under the sharia.

An exclusive military approach would not be the right way to counter its radical ideology. Alshabab successes mirror the failure of their opponents to transcend the clan issue. Although Alshabab was able to capitalize on its struggle against Ethiopian forces, its ideological inflexibility and its radicalism make it vulnerable to an efficient information campaign. Their religious interpretation and their brutality should be emphasized. The suicide attack conducted by the group on 4th October 2011 that killed scores of civilians, among them students showed Alshabab's lack of concern for civilian lives.

Demonizing Alshabab is not enough. In order to gain support, the TFG should demonstrate its ability to restore order, establish security, and provide public services.

71

The reliance on international forces should be temporary and the TFG should capitalize on the support it is receiving to strengthen its capabilities. The TFG should pursue a twofold strategy: increasing its military capability and integrating armed movements and regional political entities. For the TFG, defeating Alshabab's radical ideology is not an option but a vital necessity. It might be the case for the entire region as well.

It appears that there is not currently a coordinated effort to strengthen the Somali political institutions. Each neighboring country supports a political faction, such as the Ras Kamboni group supported by Kenya and the Ahlu Suna Wal Jama'a (ASWJ) supported by Ethiopia. What is not there is a political platform under a unified authority which could guarantee unity of effort. In the event of the defeat of Alshabab, the existence of powerful armed clan-based factions supported by different countries could hinder the governmental institution building process.

The Kenyan military intervention is a testimony to the inefficiency of the strategy of using clan-based factions against Alshabab. These clan-based armed factions have achieved little against Alshabab. They were unable to unify themselves and defeat the radical movement. The kidnaping of tourists inside Kenya posed a serious risk to the main source of Kenya's economy. Thus, the Kenyan government decided to step in and do the job itself, and on 15th October 2011, its troops entered Somalia. It is yet another episode of the two decade long Somali predicament. Whether this involvement will bear fruit or not, time will tell. It would have been more politically efficient and less embarrassing for the TFG if the Kenya troops were under the command of AMISOM.

To illustrate the uneasiness of the TFG members, a week after the Kenya operation, and despite numerous media reports, no TFG official recognized the presence

72

of Kenyan troops in Somalia. Later on, the TFG president Sheikh Sharif even criticized Kenya's action. Finally, On October 31, the two countries signed an agreement on the issue.[5] Alshabab is already exploiting the situation and has called on all Somalis to resist the Kenyan invasion. More concerted efforts from neighboring countries, the African Union and Somali political entities could ensure a unity of effort, whether on a military level against Alshabab or on the political level by building an efficient governmental institutional framework.

## Summary

The Alshabab phenomenon is the result of an internal evolution of the Somali socio-political environment. This evolution was induced by internal factors such as the emergence and expansion of various Islamic movements. However, external factors such as the Global War on Terror (GWOT) and the Ethiopian military intervention strongly impacted on Somalia and created favorable conditions for further radicalization. Alshabab is a jihadist organization strongly influenced by the global jihad movement and Al Qaida rhetoric against western dominance. The movement has made territorial gains in the past due to its simplistic message that call for the unification of Somalis under sharia rule and the need to fight against foreign military presence in Somalia. Their aggressiveness has allowed them to control all southern territories previously controlled by clan-based factions. Despite their recent setbacks, Alshabab is not yet defeated. However, the movement's survival is dependent on its willingness to evolve and adopt political pragmatism as Somalis and the entire region is mobilizing against their radicalism. The question is: will Alshabab be able to change and abandon its jihadi ideology? This is a question for further study.

[1]BBC News Africa, "Somalia: P.M Mohamed Abdullahi Mohamed resigns," June 19, 2011, http://www.bbc.co.uk/news/world-africa-13830470 (accessed October 5, 2011).

[2]Shay, 51.

[3]Marchal, 20.

[4]Ibid.

[5]Laaska news.com, "Kenya and Somalia agreement," November 1, 2011, http://laaska.wordpress.com/2011/11/01/kenya-and-somalia-agreement-sonna/ (accessed November 9, 2011).

# BIBLIOGRAPHY

## Books

Abul A'la Mawdudi, Sayyid. *The Islamic Movement: Dynamics of Values, Power and Change*. Edited by Khurram Murad. Leicester, UK: The Islamic Foundation, Markfield Dawah Centre, 1998.

———. *Towards Understanding Islam*. Translated by Khurram Murad. New Delhi, India: Markazi Maktaba Islami Publishers, 2009.

An Africa Watch Report. *Somalia: A Government at war with its own people. Testimonies about the Killings and the Conflict in the North*. United States of America: The Africa Watch Committee, 1990.

Aristotle. *The Politics*. Introduction, Notes, and Glossary and Translated by Carnes Loord. Chicago: The University of Chicago Press, 1984.

Baumann, Robert F., and Lawrance A. Yale with VersalleF.Washington. *My Clan Against The World. U.S and Coalition Forces in Somalia (1992-1994)*. Fort Leavenworth, KS: Combat Studies Institute Press, 2004.

Bruton, Bronwyn E. *Somalia: A New Approach. Council Special Report No52*. New York: Council on Foreign Relations, March 2010.

Burchill, Scott, Andrew Linklater, Richard Devetak, Lack Donnelly, Terry Nardin, Matthew Paterson, Christian Reus-Smit, and Jacqui True. *Theories of International Relations*. 4th ed. New York: Palgrave Macmillan, 2009.

Creswell, John W. *Qualitative Inquiry and Research Design: Choosing Among Five Approaches*, 2nd ed. Thousand Oaks, CA: Sage Publication, 2007.

De Waal, Alex, ed., *Islamism and Its Enemies in the Horn of Africa*. Bloomington, IN: Indiana University Press, 2004.

Elmi, Afyare. *Understanding The Somali Conflagration, Identity, Political Islam and Peacebuilding*. London: Pluto Press, 2010.

Hobbes, Thomas. *Leviathan*. Mineola, NY: Dover Publications, 2006.

Ibn Arabi. *Divine Sayings: 101 Hadith Qudsi: The Mishkat Al-Anwar of Ibn'Arabi*. Translated by Stephen Hirtenstein and Martin Notcutt. Oxford, UK: Anqa Publishing, 2004.

Kamali, H. Mohamed. *A Textbook of Hadith Studies: Authenticity, compilation, classification and Criticicism of Hadith.* Markfield, Leicestershire, UK: Islamic Foundation, 2005.

———. *Shari'a Law: An Introduction.* Oxford, UK: Oneworld Publications, 2008.

Koya, K. P., ed. *Hadith and Sunna.* Kuala Lumpur, Malaysia: Islamic Book Trust, 1996.

Lewis, I. M. *Blood and Bone. The Call of Kinship in Somali Society.* Lawrenceville, NJ: The Red Sea Press, 1994.

———. *Saints and Somali: Popular Islam in a Clan-Based Society.* Lawrenceville, NJ: The Red Sea Press, 1998.

Lyons, Terrance, and Ahmed I. Samatar. *Somalia: State Collapse, Multilateral Intervention, and Strategies for Political Reconstruction.* Washington, DC: Brookings Institution, 1995.

Marshall, Catherine, and Gretchen B. Rossman. *Designing Qualitative Research*, 3rd ed. London: Sage Publications, 1999.

Qutb, Seyyid. *Milestones.* Damascus, Syria: Dar Al Ilm.

Rapoport, Yossef, and Shabab Ahmed. *IbnTaymiyya and his times.* Oxford, UK: Oxford University Press, 2010.

Rotberg, I. Robert, ed. *Battling Terrorism in the Horn of Africa.* Harrisonburg, VA: World Peace Foundation, Brookings Institution Press, 2005.

Rousseau, Jean-Jacques. *The Social Contract.* Lexington, KY: Pacific Publishing Studio, 2010.

Shay, Shaul. *Somalia between Jihad and Restoration.* New Brunswick, NJ: Transaction Publishers, 2008.


Internet Sources

Abu Ibrahim. "Mad soo gaadhay Gaal iyo Wadaad Gaadh u wada tagaan" [Have you seen an infidel and a religious man together]. Amiirnuur, entry posted January 2011. http://www.amiirnuur.com/index.php?option=com_content&view=article &id=3399:ma-soo-gaadhay-gaal-iyo-wadad-gaadh-u-wada-taagan-qormadii-23-aad&catid=59:maqaallo&Itemid=86 (accessed July 1, 2011).

African Union Mission in Somalia (AMISOM). http://www.africa-union.org/root/ AU/AUC/Departments/PSC/AMISOM/amisom.htm (accessed June 28, 2011).

Associated Press. "Somalia's al-Qaeda leader killed in airstrikes." *USA Today* (May 2008). http://www.usatoday.com/news/world/2008-05-01-somalia-airstrike_N.htm?csp=34 (accessed July 1, 2011).

BBC News. "Somalia soccer shooting arrest." July 2006. http://news.bbc.co.uk/2/hi/africa/5153800.stm (accessed July 1, 2011).

———. "Somalia al-Shabab Islamist denies causing deadly bomb." December 4, 2009. http://news.bbc.co.uk/2/hi/africa/8394528.stm (accessed July 15, 2011).

BBC News Africa. "Somalia: P.M Mohamed Abdullahi Mohamed resigns." June 19, 2011. http://www.bbc.co.uk/news/world-africa-13830470 (accessed June 20, 2011).

Christopher Anzalone. "Building an Insurgent State." Hiiraan Online, March 15, 2011. http://www.hiiraan.com/op2/2011/mar/building_an_insurgent_state_in_somalia.aspx (accessed July 3, 2011).

Duale, A. Siiarag. "The Birth and Rise of Al-Ittihad Al-Islami in the Somali inhabited regions of the Horn of Africa." http://wardheernews.com/articles/November/13__Alittihad_Sii%27arag.html (accessed April 21, 2011).

Gartenstein-Ross, Daveed, and Seungwon Chung. "The African Union's beleaguered Somalia Mission." *The Long War Journal*, entry posted July 20, 2010. http://www.longwarjournal.org/archives/2010/07/the_african_unions_b.php (accessed May 17, 2011).

Gerard Prunier, chercheur au CNRS, directeur du Centre Francais des Etudes Ethiopiennes (Addis Abeba) [researcher, director of the French Center for Ethiopian Studies]. Propos recueillis par Robert Wiren [interviewed by Robert Wiren] *Les Nouvelles D'Addis* [Addis News]. http://www.lesnouvelles.org/P10_magazine/15_grandentretien/15013_gerardprunier.html (accessed June 19, 2011).

IRIN, "Somalia: The challenge of change." July 2006. http://www.irinnews.org/PrintReport.aspx?ReportId=59567 (accessed July 15, 2011).

———. "Somalia: UIC disarm militia, tightens control over Kismayo." September 2006. http://www.irinnews.org/report.aspx?reportid=61203 (accessed July 15, 2011).

Kismaayonews.com. "Interview of Mukhtar Robow by Aljazeera." translated by Sabriye Macalin Muuse. March 2009. http://kismaayonews.com/pageView.php?articleid=295 (accessed July 1, 2011).

Laaska news.com. "Kenya and Somalia agreement." November 1, 2011. http://laaska.wordpress.com/2011/11/01/kenya-and-somalia-agreement-sonna/ (accessed November 9, 2011).

Marchal, Roland. "The Rise of A Jihadi Movement in a Country at War: Harakat Al-Shabaab Al Mujaheddin in Somalia." http://www.ceri-sciences-po.org/ressource/shabaab.pdf (accessed June 20, 2011).

McGuie, Meredith Preston. "Mediating Djibouti." Conciliation Resources, 2010. http://www.c-r.org/our-work/accord/somalia/mediating-djibouti.php (accessed June 11, 2011).

Menkhaus, Kenneth J. "Political Islam in Somalia." http://www.somali-jna.org/downloads/Menkhaus%20-%20Political%20Islam%20in%20Somalia.pdf (accessed April 20, 2011).

Najad Abdullahi. "Toxic Waste behind Somali Piracy." Al Jazeera English, October 2008. http://english.aljazeera.net/news/africa/2008/10/2008109174223218644.html (accessed July 3, 2011).

Radio Shabelle. "Shabaab iyo ganacsato isku raacay inay la dagaalamaan DKMG" [Alshabab and businessmen agreed to resist to TFG]. Radio Shabelle, May 2011. http://shabelle.net/article.php?id=7054 (accessed July 15, 2011).

Radiomogadisho. "Taariikhda Axmed Godane" [Biography of Ahmad Godane]. radiomogadisho, May 12, 2011. http://radiomuqdisho.net/taariikhda-axmed-godane-dhagayso/ (accessed May 25, 2011).

Roggio, Bill. "Shabaab suicide attack kills 20 in Somali capital." *The Long War Journal*, February 22, 2011. http://www.longwarjournal.org/archives/2011/02/shabaab_suicide_atta_1.php (accessed June 7, 2011)

Security Council. SC/10139, "Security Council extends authorization of African Union Mission in Somalia until 30 September 2011." December 22, 2010. http://www.un.org/News/Press/docs/2010/sc10139.doc.htm (accessed June 15, 2011).

————. SC/8960, "Security Council Authorizes Six-Month African Union Mission in Somalia." United Nations, Department of Public Information News and Media Division, February 20, 2007. http://www.un.org/News/Press/docs/2007/sc8960.doc.htm (accessed June 15, 2011).

Shinn, David H. "Al-Qaeda, Al-Shabaab and Somalia." *Mashriq Quarterly Magazine* (February 2011). http://mashriqq.com/?p=1790 (accessed July 15, 2011).

*The Somaliland Times*. "Khat Fight in Somalia Question Islamist Position." no. 252. http://www.somalilandtimes.net/sl/2006/252/091.shtml (accessed July 1, 2011).

Torill Moen. "Reflections on the Narrative Research Approach." *International Journal of Qualitative Methods* (December 5, 2006). http://www.ualberta.ca/~iiqm/backissues/5_4/HTML/moen.htm (accessed September 15, 2011).

Voice of America, "Djibouti to soon send Peacekeepers to Somalia," May 14, 2011. http://blogs.voanews.com/breaking-news/2011/05/14/djibouti-to-soon-send-peacekeepers-to-somalia (accessed June 30, 2011).